HAMLET

William Shakespeare

AUTHORED by Marty O'Kane
UPDATED AND REVISED by Elizabeth Weinbloom

COVER DESIGN by Table XI Partners LLC
COVER PHOTO by Olivia Verma and © 2005 GradeSaver, LLC

BOOK DESIGN by Table XI Partners LLC

Published by GradeSaver LLC, www.gradesaver.com

First published in the United States of America by GradeSaver LLC. 2013

ISBN 978-1-60259-377-0

Printed in the United States of America

For other products and additional information please visit http://www.gradesaver.com

Table of Contents

Table of Contents

Table of Contents

Table of Contents

Teaching Guide - About the Author

William Shakespeare is arguably the most famous writer of the English language, known for both his plays and sonnets. Though much about his life remains open to speculation due to incomplete evidence, the following biography consolidates the most widely-accepted facts of his life and career.

Born in the idyllic town of Stratford-upon-Avon, William Shakespeare was the third child of the former Mary Arden and John Shakespeare, a successful tradesman and local politician. His birth is unregistered, but legend pins it on April 23, 1564, possibly because it is known that April 23 is the day on which he died 52 years later. Little is known about Shakespeare's childhood, although it is generally assumed that he attended the local grammar school, the King's New School. The school was staffed by Oxford-educated faculty who taught the students mathematics, natural sciences, logic, Christian ethics, and classical language and literature.

Shakespeare did not attend university, which was not at all unusual for the time. University education was reserved for wealthy sons of the elite, mostly those who wanted to become clergymen. The numerous classical and literary references in Shakespeare's plays are a testament, therefore to the excellent education he received in grammar school (and to his ability as an autodidact). His early plays in particular draw on the works of Seneca and Plautus. Even more impressive than his formal education is the wealth of general knowledge exhibited in his works. His vocabulary exceeds that of any other English writer by a wide margin.

In 1582, at the age of eighteen, William Shakespeare married the twenty-six-year-old Anne Hathaway. Their first daughter, Susanna, was baptized only six months later—a fact that has given rise to speculation over the circumstances surrounding their marriage. In 1585, Anne bore twins, baptized Hamnet and Judith Shakespeare. Hamnet died at the age of eleven, by which time Shakespeare was already a successful playwright. Around 1589, Shakespeare wrote what is considered his first play, Henry VI, Part 1. Sometime between his marriage and writing this play, he moved to London, where he pursued a career as a playwright and actor.

Although many records of Shakespeare's life as a citizen of Stratford—including marriage and birth certificates—have survived, very little information exists about his life as a young playwright. Legend characterizes Shakespeare as a roguish young man who was once forced to flee London under suspect circumstances, perhaps having to do with his love life. But the paltry amount of written information does not necessarily confirm this characterization.

In any case, young Will was not an immediate and universal success. The earliest written record of Shakespeare's life in London comes from a statement by the rival playwright Robert Greene. In his Groatsworth of Witte (1592), Greene calls Shakespeare an "upstart crow...[who] supposes he is as well able to bombast out a blank verse as the best of you." While this is hardly high praise, it does suggest that Shakespeare rattled the London theatrical hierarchy even at the beginning of his career. It is natural, in retrospect, to attribute Greene's complaint to jealousy of Shakespeare's ability, but there is little evidence one way or the other.

With Richard III, Henry VI, The Comedy of Errors, and Titus Andronicus under his belt, Shakespeare was a popular playwright by 1590.* The year 1593, however, marked a major leap forward in his career. By the end of that year, he secured a prominent patron in the Earl of Southampton, and his Venus and Adonis was published. It remains one of the first of his known works to be printed, and was a huge success. Next came The Rape of Lucrece. Shakespeare had also made his mark as a poet, and most scholars agree that the majority of Shakespeare's sonnets were probably written in the 1590s.

In 1594, Shakespeare returned to the theater and became a charter member of the Lord Chamberlain's Men—a group of actors who changed their name to the King's Men when James I ascended to the throne. By 1598, he was the "principal comedian" for the troupe; by 1603, he was "principal tragedian." He remained associated with the organization until his death. Although acting and playwriting were not considered noble professions at the time, successful and prosperous actors were relatively well respected. Shakespeare's success left him with a fair amount of money, which he invested in Stratford real estate. In 1597, he purchased the second largest house in Stratford—the New Place—for his parents. In 1596, Shakespeare applied for a coat of arms for his family, in effect making himself a gentleman. Consequently, his daughters made "good matches," and married wealthy men.

The same year that he joined the Lord Chamberlain's Men, Shakespeare wrote Romeo and Juliet, along with Love's Labour's Lost, The Taming of the Shrew, and several other plays. Two of his greatest tragedies, Hamlet and Julius Caesar, followed around 1600. Hamlet is widely considered the first modern play for its multi-faceted main character and unprecedented depiction of the human psyche.

The first decade of the seventeenth century witnessed the debut performances of many of Shakespeare's most celebrated works, including many of his so-called history plays: Othello in 1604 or 1605; Antony and Cleopatra in 1606 or 1607; and King Lear in 1608. The last of his plays to be performed was probably King Henry VIII in either 1612 or 1613.

William Shakespeare lived until 1616. His wife Anna died in 1623, at the age of 67. He was buried in the chancel of his church at Stratford. The lines above his tomb—allegedly written by Shakespeare himself—read:

Good friend, for Jesus' sake forbear

To dig the dust enclosed here.

Blessed be the man that spares these stones

And cursed be he that moves my bones.

*The dates of composition and performance of almost all of Shakespeare's plays remain uncertain. The dates used in this note are widely agreed upon by scholars, but significant debate around when and where he wrote most of his plays persists.

Teaching Guide - Study Objectives

If all of the elements of this lesson plan are employed, students will develop the following powers, skills, and understanding:

1. In both writing and classroom discussions, students will form and defend their own opinions about the text's meaning, citing specific textual evidence or inferences drawn from the text to defend these opinions. In areas where the text might be vague or inconclusive, students will use textual evidence, their knowledge of history and literature, and their own personal experience to form reasoned conjectures.

2. Students will gain a greater understanding of and appreciation for: figurative language (including similes and extended metaphors), wordplay, irony, and classical rhetorical devices.

3. Students will build vocabulary through various techniques, including using context and consulting reference materials.

4. Students will learn how different presentations of a dramatic work - either through different staging or different types of media - affect its overall meaning.

Teaching Guide - Common Core Standards

- 11-12 - CCSS.ELA-Literacy.CCRA.R.1 Read closely to determine what the text says explicitly and to make logical inferences from it; cite specific textual evidence when writing or speaking to support conclusions drawn from the text.

- 11-12 - CCSS.ELA-Literacy.CCRA.R.3 Analyze how and why individuals, events, or ideas develop and interact over the course of a text.

- 11-12 - CCSS.ELA-Literacy.CCRA.R.6 Assess how point of view or purpose shapes the content and style of a text.

- 11-12 - CCSS.ELA-Literacy.CCRA.L.4 Determine or clarify the meaning of unknown and multiple-meaning words and phrases by using context clues, analyzing meaningful word parts, and consulting general and specialized reference materials, as appropriate.

- 11-12 - CCSS.ELA-Literacy.CCRA.R.7 Integrate and evaluate content presented in diverse media and formats, including visually and quantitatively, as well as in words.

- 11-12 - CCSS.ELA-Literacy.CCRA.W.1 Write arguments to support claims in an analysis of substantive topics or texts using valid reasoning and relevant and sufficient evidence.

- 11-12 - CCSS.ELA-Literacy.CCRA.SL.4 Present information, findings, and supporting evidence such that listeners can follow the line of reasoning and the organization, development, and style are appropriate to task, purpose, and audience.

- 11-12 - CCSS.ELA-Literacy.CCRA.SL.1 Prepare for and participate effectively in a range of conversations and collaborations with diverse partners, building on others' ideas and expressing their own clearly and persuasively.

- 11-12 - CCSS.ELA-Literacy.CCRA.L.3 Apply knowledge of language to understand how language functions in different contexts, to make effective choices for meaning or style, and to comprehend more fully when reading or listening.

- 11-12 - CCSS.ELA-Literacy.CCRA.L.4 Determine or clarify the meaning of unknown and multiple-meaning words and phrases by using context clues, analyzing meaningful word parts, and consulting general and specialized reference materials, as appropriate.

- 11-12 - CCSS.ELA-Literacy.CCRA.L.5 Demonstrate understanding of figurative language, word relationships, and nuances in word meanings.

Teaching Guide - Introduction to Hamlet

Alongside the *King James Bible*, *Hamlet* may be the most influential text in the history of the English language. Even those who have never read nor seen the play have at least a passing familiarity with its most iconic scenes, and with the numerous phrases it has introduced to the popular lexicon, including "primrose path," "cruel to be kind," "method in madness," "to be or not to be," "woe is me," "brevity is the soul of wit," and "to thine own self be true," to name but a few.

Part of the play's enduring legacy is that it comments so eloquently on elements that are at the center of the human experience: death and afterlife, love and family, honor and revenge, melancholy and madness. Another part of its lasting appeal is the power and mystery of its main character. With *Hamlet*, Shakespeare subverted the ancient Aristotelian model of drama by emphasizing character development over plot, and in doing so, created what is considered by many to be the first antihero, and the first "modern" drama. So advanced are Shakespeare's observations on human nature and existence in *Hamlet* that they continue to challenge and confound critics at the highest level of literary analysis, over four hundred years after they were first published.

Key Aspects of Hamlet

Tone

Aside from a few instances of comic relief, most notably the gravedigger scene, the mood of *Hamlet* shifts between gloomy, melancholic introspection, heartbreaking scenes of grief, and violent outbursts of passionate anger.

Setting

The action of the play takes place in and around Elsinore Castle in Denmark at some unspecified time during the Medieval era. Befitting the dark subject matter of the play, Elsinore is a place of isolation, shadows, and secret places. It is a place where the cunning and the deceitful rise to the top, while the innocent are manipulated by those in power.

Point of View

As a play, *Hamlet* offers us neither a first-person nor an omniscient third-person point of view. In many ways, this adds to the play's power, because it leaves the interpretation of the characters' motivations and actions up to the audience itself. One of the more interesting devices of *Hamlet* is that it often involves a character or characters observing the actions of other characters in secret, offering the audience two perspectives on the same scene, thus heightening the scene's dramatic irony and tension.

Character Development

Over the course of the play, Hamlet passes through what could be considered a variation on the "stages of grief": when we first encounter him, he is in the depths of an intense melancholy brought on by his father's death and his mother's marriage to Claudius. There is, of course, an undercurrent of rage beneath this depression, one that boils to the surface with the ghost's revelation of Claudius' crimes. Hamlet's incessant philosophizing and the contrivance of the play-within-a-play can be seen as a type of "bargaining", which give way to the serene acceptance of his fate he demonstrates in the play's final act.

Claudius begins the play as a capable ruler and as a seemingly caring stepfather, but as revealed in his soliloquy in Act III, he is a man who is crumbling under the weight of his numerous sins. (It is worth noting that Claudius is the only character aside from Hamlet to deliver a soliloquy during the play). Once he realizes that he is in danger of being exposed, Claudius descends into complete villainy; his scheming ultimately results in his own death, along with the deaths of Hamlet, Gertrude, and Laertes.

Gertrude, while one of the central figures of the play, is also one of the most enigmatic. Despite the seething resentment Hamlet holds toward her, Gertrude appears to be a caring and affectionate mother. Her role in Old Hamlet's death and her previous relationship with Claudius is open to various interpretations. Whatever it was, she bitterly regrets her subsequent actions in her confrontation with Hamlet in Act III.

Ophelia undergoes the most radical transformation in the play. Throughout much of the play's action, she serves as a counterpoint to Hamlet's exaggerated misogyny. While Hamlet views women as faithless and manipulative, Ophelia is the very picture of obedience and loyalty. Following her father's murder at the hands of the man who repudiated her love, Ophelia suffers a complete mental collapse. Her madness is at once one of the most pathetic and intriguing aspects of the play, and her tragic death sets in motion the events that lead to the play's final confrontation.

Since all we know of the remaining characters is revealed through dialogue (not soliloquies), the characterizations of the remaining characters remain somewhat fixed: the steadfast and stalwart Horatio, the foolish, officious Polonius, the grim, martial Fortinbras, and the fungible Rosencrantz and Guildenstern.

Themes

Revenge

The revenge play was a popular dramatic form in Elizabethan England, and Shakespeare adopted many of its conventions for *Hamlet*: a secret murder, a supernatural encounter, feigned madness, and a bloody climax in which both the protagonist and antagonist are killed. However, Shakespeare expanded upon these conventions by adding a more complex moral and psychological dimension to his revenge tale. More than just an exercise in revenge wish fulfillment, *Hamlet* is an exploration of what constitutes a just revenge. The ghost's pathetic fate makes us want Hamlet to pay his uncle in kind, but the player's portrayal of Pyrrhus' bloody murder of Priam reminds us that revenge is an act that can defile its seeker just as much as it destroys its victim. In contrast to his impulsive counterparts Laertes and Fortinbras, Hamlet seeks a vengeance that will allow him to punish Claudius without compromising his moral code. Hamlet's dithering and self-examination may thus frustrate the reader at times, but his insistence on making sure his revenge is justly served makes it ultimately more satisfying in the end.

Death

Death pervades the action of *Hamlet*, from the ghostly visitation of its opening to the bloody "havoc" of its final scene. Throughout the play, but most especially in the graveyard scene, the audience is confronted by the inevitability and finality of death. On more than one occasion, Hamlet observes that, regardless of our station in this life, in the end we all die, decay, and return to the earth. At the same time, *Hamlet* deals with the unfathomable mystery of what follows death, as personified by the character of the ghost, and so eloquently expressed in Hamlet's "To be or not to be" soliloquy. It is the mystery of the true nature of death the drives much of Hamlet's philosophical speculation, and prevents him from murdering Claudius at his most propitious opportunity.

Appearance vs. Reality

One of the more compelling features of *Hamlet* is the way it intertwines the realms of theater and reality. This is most evident in the inclusion of the play-within-a-play, and in Hamlet's commentary on the player's ability to summon genuine emotion over a fictional conceit. But in a way, all of *Hamlet* could be considered a play-within-a-play. At some point or another, its main characters inhabit "roles" that mask their real intentions, and much of the play's action involves one character "stage directing" the other characters, either to provoke a particular response or to achieve a particular end. One of the play's messages is that while theater is a reflection of reality, reality itself involves a certain degree of theatricality. As Hamlet points out in Act I, there is a sharp division between one's outward persona – the way one "seems" – and one's truest self – that "which passeth show". The tension and interplay between these two halves is explored throughout the play.

Madness and Melancholy

Closely tied to the play's theme of appearance vs. reality is its depiction of madness and melancholy. Hamlet's true mental state is one of the play's unsolved riddles. As a character dealing with his father's death and his mother's "o'erhasty marriage," Hamlet is genuinely melancholy at the beginning of the play, and this depression colors the mood of the entire play. Whether this melancholy degenerates into full-blown madness is the subject of some debate. We know that Hamlet deliberately feigns madness at some points, and admits to doing so. However, there seems to be something more than affectation in his harsh treatment of Ophelia, who laments a "noble mind... o'erthrown." It is Hamlet's rejection of her love, combined with the loss of her father, that causes Ophelia's madness, the reality of which seems far from doubt. In the case of both Hamlet's feigned and Ophelia's genuine madness, those observing it marvel as its power to convey emotional truths that are, as Laertes says, "more than matter." Thus, *Hamlet* portrays madness as at once a debilitating yet strangely liberating force.

Power and Corruption

The characters who represent the political power structure of Hamlet's Denmark – Claudius, Polonius, Osric – are presented at best as simpering, sycophantic fools, and at worst as deceitful, murdering villains. On the other hand, the representatives of the more humble classes – Horatio, Ophelia, Marcellus, Bernardo – are portrayed as being ceaselessly loyal, humble, and gracious. Horatio, in particular, is singled out by Hamlet for specific praise for his honorable stoicism and good nature. The message, common to many of Shakespeare's plays, is that the acquisition and maintenance of power requires a certain degree of deviousness and artificiality.

Symbols

Hamlet's clothes: At the beginning of the play, Hamlet is still in black mourning dress over the loss of his father, who has been dead for two months. As Hamlet himself points out, this "inky cloak" reflects a deeper darkness that he holds within himself.

Yorick's skull: Represents the inevitability and permanence of death, and reinforces the idea that regardless of our station in life, in the end we all meet the same fate.

The Ghost: One of the more perplexing characters of *Hamlet*, the Ghost represents the mystery of what lies beyond death, and thus personifies one of the main themes of the play.

Climax

As with most of Shakespeare's plays, *Hamlet* reaches its climax in its third act, when Hamlet murders Polonius during a heated confrontation with his mother. This act sets in motion a chain of events - Hamlet's banishment, Laertes' return, Ophelia's death and burial - that culminates in the duel between Hamlet and Laertes in Act V, in which most of the remaining principals meet their ends.

Structure

Hamlet is divided into five acts, each containing between two to seven scenes. At 3834 lines, it is Shakespeare's longest play.

Teaching Guide - Relationship with Other Books

With its focus on revenge and the corrosive influence of power, and its inclusion of supernatural elements, *Hamlet* most closely resembles *Macbeth*, *Julius Caesar*, and *The Tempest* among Shakespeare's works. Shakespeare also touches upon the subject of revenge in *Othello* and *Titus Andronicus*, and the theme of madness is central to *King Lear*. The inclusion of a ghostly visitation in a common Shakespearean device; along with *Macbeth* and *Julius Caesar*, it is also featured prominently in *Cymbeline* and *Richard III.*

Hamlet's theme of revenge is at the core of numerous works, including *Paradise Lost*, *Moby Dick*, *The Count of Monte Cristo*, *Great Expectations*, and "The Cask of Amontillado", while the subject of madness is confronted in works such as *A Streetcar Named Desire*, *One Flew Over the Cuckoo's Nest*, and *Girl, Interrupted.*

In his adoption of a false persona to cover his true intentions, Hamlet bears some similarity to the character of Jay Gatsby in Fitzgerald's *The Great Gatsby*, and Hamlet and Horatio's friendship has much in common with that of Gatsby and Nick Carraway.

Dante's *The Divine Comedy* provides a broader picture of the cosmological backdrop of *Hamlet*, and elaborates on the system of divine retribution that informs Hamlet's actions.

References to *Hamlet* itself abound in western culture, from high literature such as Eliot's "The Love Song of J. Alfred Prufrock", Joyce's *Ulysses*, and Wallace's *Infinite Jest* to pop culture fare such as *The Empire Strikes Back* and *The Lion King*. It has also provided a popular target for parody, in plays such as Tom Stoppard's *Rosencrantz and Guilendstern Are Dead* and Paul Rudnick's *I Hate Hamlet*, and on television shows such as *Monty Python's Flying Circus* and *The Simpsons.*

Teaching Guide - Bringing In Technology

In order for students to fully appreciate Shakespeare's work, they must be able to view it in performance. Several of the activities included in this lesson plan involve comparisons of different adaptations of *Hamlet*, so you will need to secure the appropriate technology for classroom viewing (DVD or Internet) before the first activity.

A number of the group exercises involve some sort of performance element. These exercises were designed to be performed in the classroom, but if students have access to video recording and editing technology, you can encourage them to submit their work as video projects. Even if students decide to perform these activities in the classroom, their structure is flexible enough to allow students to incorporate different forms of A/V technology (smart boards, Power Point, pre-recorded music and/or video, etc).

Hamlet has a long and robust history of adaptation. You may wish to have students read, watch, perform, or play some of the many versions, such as Seamus Kennedy's "The Three Minute Hamlet" at http://www.youtube.com/watch?v=e31bOXbDyog, the *Hamlet* text adventure game at http://rdouglasjohnson.com/hamlet/, or the *Hamlet* section of *The Complete Works of William Shakespeare, Abridged.* You might also want to incorporate technology in having students create their own adaptations, whether as movies, recorded theater, podcasts, or more.

Teaching Guide - Notes to the Teacher

Every classroom is different, but the key to teaching a play, whether it is in a literature course or a drama or theater course, is to bring the play alive in your classroom. Reading a play is a different experience from reading a novel; likewise, a play should be taught differently. This lesson plan includes activities and questions that can be used to encourage students to perform and see the play as a performative text.

Remember that some students will have a limited theatrical background, while others will be experienced actors. Cast accordingly. Do not suggest that those with no background are going to have a harder time earning a good grade, but do point out that the more reading and watching and performing they do, the easier it will be to understand and appreciate the performing arts in the future. Virtually all of them will have viewed a lot of acting and dramatic art, whether on television or at the movies, and they can be counted on to view a lot more of it in the future. Now is a chance for them to refine and deepen their powers of comprehending and appreciating what they see.

The thought questions in this lesson plan provide material and ideas that students can use to write short original essays and to develop their powers of thought. For the sake of improving the power of expression, teachers should encourage students to write on topics that have been discussed in class, this time in the more formal writing style expected in a literary essay. At the same time, students should not be discouraged from choosing their own topics.

The questions provided for the final paper are most suitable for student essays. Remember that grading an essay should not depend on a simple checklist of required content.

Author of Lesson Plan and Sources

Marty O'Kane, author of Lesson Plan. Completed on August 07, 2013, copyright held by GradeSaver.

Updated and revised Elizabeth Weinbloom August 26, 2013. Copyright held by GradeSaver.

William Shakespeare. Hamlet. New York: Signet Classic, 1998.

Folger Shakespeare Library. "Folger Shakespeare Library." 2013-07-15. <http://www.folger.edu>.

"Hamlet Line Count." 2013-07-20. <https://sites.google.com/a/shakespearelinecount.com/www/hamlet-characters>.

Royal Shakespeare Company. "Hamlet Teachers' Guide." 2013-07-01. <http://www-tc.pbs.org/wnet/gperf/files/2010/04/Hamlet-Teachers-Guide.pdf>.

"The Tragedy of Hamlet, Prince of Denmark." 2013-07-06. <http://shakespeare.mit.edu/hamlet/full.html>.

Mabillard, Amanda, et al.. "Hamlet Study Guide." 2013-07-10. <http://www.shakespeare-online.com/plays/hamlet/hamletresources.html>.

"Hamlet." 2013-06-30. <http://en.wikipedia.org/wiki/Hamlet>.

"Hamlet and Polonius ("words, words")." 2013-07-01. <http://www.youtube.com/watch?v=l93LR6Sw75Q>.

Barnet, Sylvan. "Shakespeare: An Overview." *Hamlet.* Ed. Sylvan Barnet. New York: Signet Classic. pp. vii-lxi

Barnet, Sylvan. "Introduction to *Hamlet.*" i[Hamlet.] Ed. Sylvan Barnet. New York: Signet Classic. pp. vii-lxi

Olivier, Laurence, dir. *Hamlet.* Rank Film Distributors Ltd, 1948. Film.

Zeffirelli, Franco, dir. *Hamlet.* Warner Bros, 1990. Film.

Branagh, Kenneth, dir. *Hamlet.* Columbia Pictures, 1996. Film.

"Hamlet." *Great Performances.* PBS. Dir. Gregory Doran. 28 April 2010. Television.

Related Links

http://shakespeare.mit.edu/hamlet/full.html
The Tragedy of Hamlet, Prince of Denmark The full text of *Hamlet*, provided by the Massachusetts Institute of Technology.

http://www.folger.edu/?gclid=CMO6k8vWm7kCFRM72woddlQAcw
The Folger Shakespeare Library Contains a wealth of Shakespeare resources and support materials.

http://www.bardweb.net/
Shakespeare Resource Center Features links to numerous sites devoted to the life and work of William Shakespeare.

http://www.shakespeareinamericancommunities.org/education
Shakespeare in American Communities Contains information on the playwright himself, the Elizabethan period in which he lived and wrote, Shakespeare in America, and much more.

http://www.greekmythology.com/
Greek Mythology A quick but comprehensive resource for additional information on the numerous gods, heroes, and classical works referenced in Shakespeare's works.

http://www.shakespearesglobe.com/
Shakespeare's Globe The official web site of Shakespeare's Globe, a recreation of the original Globe Theatre, where many of Shakespeare's works were first performed.

Day 1 - Reading Assignment

Read Act I.

Common Core Objectives

- CCSS.ELA-Literacy.CCRA.R.1 Read closely to determine what the text says explicitly and to make logical inferences from it; cite specific textual evidence when writing or speaking to support conclusions drawn from the text.
- CCSS.ELA-Literacy.CCRA.R.3 Analyze how and why individuals, events, or ideas develop and interact over the course of a text.
- CCSS.ELA-Literacy.CCRA.R.6 Assess how point of view or purpose shapes the content and style of a text.

Note that it is perfectly fine to expand any day's work into two days depending on the characteristics of the class, particularly if the class will engage in all of the suggested classroom exercises and activities and discuss all of the thought questions.

Content Summary for Teachers

Act I:

Through expository dialogue in its first scene, Act I provides us with the backstory for *Hamlet*: Denmark's warrior king, Old Hamlet, has died suddenly, the victim of an apparent snakebite. His grieving son, Prince Hamlet, has returned from his studies at Wittenberg to attend his father's funeral. As the nobles mourn, the common folk are making feverish preparations for war with Norway, where Fortinbras, son of the dead king's vanquished foe, has raised an army with the intent of avenging his father's death.

The play opens on a dark and freezing night at Elsinore Castle, as two guardsmen take their posts. For two nights prior, their watch has been interrupted by the appearance of a ghost in the form of Old Hamlet. On this third night, they have convinced their companion Horatio to join them, to confirm that what they have seen is real. Just as Horatio expresses his skepticism, the ghost appears before them. The terrified trio tries to engage the ghost, but it will not speak to them. Thinking this visitation an ill omen for the state of Denmark, Horatio decides he must reveal what he has seen to his friend Hamlet.

In the palace shortly thereafter, a muted wedding celebration takes place. Claudius, the brother of the dead king, has not only ascended to Old Hamlet's throne, but has also wedded his widow, Gertrude. After giving leave to Laertes, son of his councilor Polonius, to return to school in France, Claudius dispatches ambassadors to the king of Norway to halt Fortinbras' advance. The newlyweds then turn their attention to

Hamlet, still in mourning clothes over the loss of his father. They implore him to cast off his "unmanly" grief, and to remain with them at Elsinore. Hamlet halfheartedly agrees, but once alone, he vents his revulsion of his stepfather/uncle, and his rage at his mother's apparent falseness. His brooding is interrupted by Horatio, who enters with news of the ghost's visitation. Engrossed by his story, Hamlet resolves to accompany Horatio and the guards on their watch that evening, in the hopes of speaking to the ghost himself.

In another part of the castle, Laertes bids farewell to his sister Ophelia, and leaves her with a stern warning: no matter how she and Hamlet might feel about each other, she must not encourage his affections. As a prince, Hamlet can play at love, but ultimately he must marry another royal; as a woman, Ophelia must do all she can to uphold her chastity. After Laertes leaves, Polonius echoes his comments, but goes a step further: from this day forward, she must have no contact with Hamlet. Ophelia humbly obeys.

That night, the ghost appears before Hamlet and his companions, and beckons Hamlet to follow him to a space apart from the others. Once they are alone, the ghost reveals that he is indeed his father's spirit, doomed to spend his days in fiery punishment to atone for his sins. Worse yet, he was brought to this torment not by a snakebite, but by his own brother's treachery: as the king slept in his orchard, Claudius murdered him by pouring poison into his ear. The ghost urges Hamlet to avenge this foul murder, and Hamlet eagerly agrees. When his companions find him after the ghost departs, Hamlet makes them swear not to reveal what they have seen, and hints at the strange behavior he will adopt to conceal his knowledge of Claudius' crimes.

Thought Questions (students consider while they read)

1. How do the setting, dialogue, and events of Scene 1 help set the mood for the rest of the play?
2. Reread Hamlet's speech in lines 76-86. How does this speech help establish on the play's main themes?
3. Consider Ophelia's conversations with Laertes and Polonius in scene 3. What advice do they give her? What do their exchanges tell you about the role of gender and class in the world of *Hamlet*?
4. Who are the most powerful characters in *Hamlet*'s Denmark? How would you describe these characters? How might these characters be a commentary on the nature of power?
5. Consider the character of the ghost. Why do you think he talks only to Hamlet? Do there seem to be any inconsistencies in his story? Why do you think he swears Hamlet and his friends to secrecy? As Hamlet himself asks, is it possible that this ghost is a demon, and not an angel?

Vocabulary (in order of appearance)

Sc. i, l. 31:

- Assail: attack

Sc. i, l. 46:

- Usurp: assume a position of power illegally; overthrow

Sc. i, l. 96:

- Mettle: courage; resilience

Sc. i, l. 109:

- Portentous: like a portent; bearing an omen; foreshadowing things to come

Sc. ii, l. 12:

- Dirge: mournful song, normally associated with funerals

Sc. ii, l. 92:

- Obsequious: related to obsequies (funerals); excessively obedient or servile

Sc. ii, l. 93:

- Obstinate: stubborn, inflexible

Sc. i, l. 94:

- Impious: irreligious, unholy

Sc. ii, l. 22:

- Circumscribed: set within particular limits

Sc. ii, l. 42:

- Imminent: unavoidable, inevitable

Sc. iv, l. 48:

- Sepulcher: tomb

Sc. v, l. 65:

- Enmity: mutual ill will; hatred

Sc. v, l. 94:

- Sinew: muscle, tissue

Sc. v, l. 178:

- Ambiguous: vague, uncertain, open to interpretation

Sc. v, l. 181:

- Perturbed: disturbed, anxious

Additional Homework

1. The afterlife that the ghost describes in Act I closely resembles the Roman Catholic concept of Purgatory. In an independent research project, study how this concept developed over the centuries. At time same time, read up on the religious climate of England around the time *Hamlet* was first written and performed (c. 1600). Why would it have been very controversial, if not downright dangerous, for Shakespeare to present a play featuring references to Purgatory to an English audience?

Day 1 - Discussion of Thought Questions

1. How do the setting, dialogue, and events of Scene 1 help set the mood for the rest of the play?

   Time: 5 min.

   Discussion: Set on a dark, freezing night on which three terrified men encounter a ghost, scene 1 establishes the mood of foreboding, tension, and uncertainty that runs throughout Hamlet. It is worth noting that the first line of the play is a question ("Who's there?"), one that deals with uncertainty and identity. As Horatio himself points out, the appearance of the ghost is a sign of an impending calamity, and is representative of one of the play's central themes - death.

2. Reread Hamlet's speech in lines 76-86. How does this speech help establish on the play's main themes?

   Time: 5 min.

   Discussion: In this speech, Hamlet draws a distinction between his outward signs of grief, which "a man might play," and his inner grief, which is more real than all of these, and surpasses them in darkness. In this speech, Hamlet establishes the theme of appearance vs. reality; throughout the play, there are characters (Hamlet included) who adopt different personae - wear "other clothes," as it were - to hide their true feelings or motivations.

3. Consider Ophelia's conversations with Laertes and Polonius in scene 3. What advice do they give her? What do their exchanges tell you about the role of gender and class in the world of *Hamlet*?

   Time: 5 min.

   Discussion: Laertes and Polonius both advise Ophelia that even if Hamlet protests his love to her, she should avoid a romantic relationship with him.

He is, after all, a prince, and no matter where his affections might tend, he ultimately must accept whatever royal marriage is arranged for him. What's more, as a man, he has more leave to be sexually adventurous than Ophelia, who must protect her chastity. If Ophelia gives into her desires, they argue, Hamlet will abandon her, and leave her open to scorn and slander. In other words, the men of *Hamlet* (especially noblemen) are given a "larger tether" to be bold and reckless, while women of *Hamlet* are expected to uphold higher standards of chastity and obedience.

4. Who are the most powerful characters in *Hamlet*'s Denmark? How would you describe these characters? How might these characters be a commentary on the nature of power?

   Time: 5 min.

   Discussion: The most powerful characters in *Hamlet*'s Denmark, at least in the temporal sense, are Claudius and Polonius. By the end of Act I, we learn that while Claudius plays the benign and reluctant monarch, he is actually a murdering usurper. Polonius, though a caring father, is also an officious and affected bureaucrat. Together, their characters convey a sense that obtaining and maintaining power requires a certain amount of ruthlessness and deception.

5. Consider the character of the ghost. Why do you think he talks only to Hamlet? Do there seem to be any inconsistencies in his story? Why do you think he swears Hamlet and his friends to secrecy? As Hamlet himself asks, is it possible that this ghost is a demon, and not an angel?

   Time: 5 min.

   Discussion: Answers for this question will vary, and you should encourage contrasting viewpoints. The point of this question is the reinforcement of the fact that *Hamlet* is in some ways made more compelling by its ambiguities, since these ambiguities allow more room for interpretation on the part of actors, directors, and audiences.

Day 1 - Short Answer Quiz

1. Where does *Hamlet* take place?

____

2. What happens to Marcellus and Bernardo on their watch?

____

3. At the beginning of the play, tensions are growing between Denmark and what country?

____

4. Laertes asks Claudius' permission to do what?

____

5. Aside from his father's death, what else is troubling Hamlet in Act I?

____

6. How do Hamlet and Horatio know each other?

____

7. Laertes tells Ophelia that she can never marry Hamlet. Why not?

---

8. Hamlet expresses his disgust for a particular Danish custom. What is it?

---

9. How did Old Hamlet die?

---

10. What oath does Hamlet ask his companions to swear?

Short Answer Quiz Key

1. Elsinore Castle, Denmark
2. They encounter a ghost.
3. Norway
4. Return to school in France.
5. His mother's marriage to his uncle Claudius.
6. They are both students at the University of Wittenberg.
7. Since Hamlet is the heir to the throne, his marriage must be arranged.
8. Drinking to excess.
9. He was murdered by his brother Claudius.
10. Not to reveal what they know about the ghost.

Day 1 - Crossword Puzzle

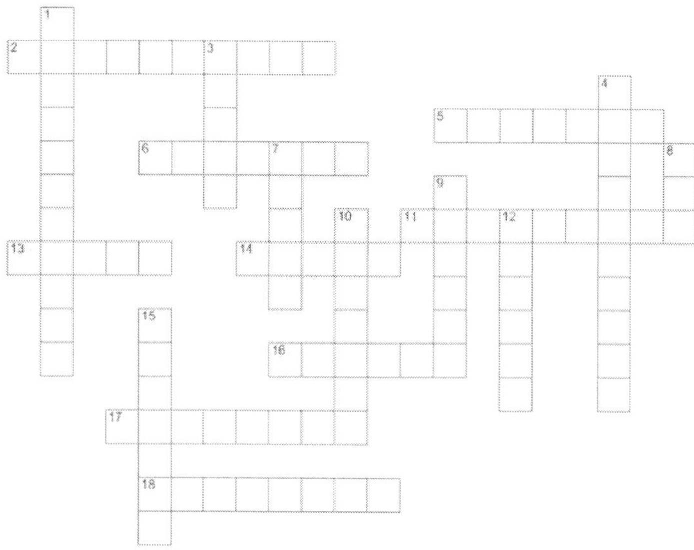

ACROSS

2. Marching against Denmark
5. Hamlet's paramour
6. Site of Old Hamlet's murder
11. Mid-sized club D
13. Light oath, or to wed
14. River in Hades
16. Hamlet's rank
17. Fanfare of trumpets
18. Hamlet setting

DOWN

1. "face" or "attention"
3. Hamlet's preferred color
4. Hamlet's alma mater
7. Farewell
8. "A little more than ____, and less than kind!"
9. Leartes attends school here
10. A type of wine
12. Cornelius' destination
15. "O that this too too ________ flesh would melt"

Crossword Puzzle Answer Key

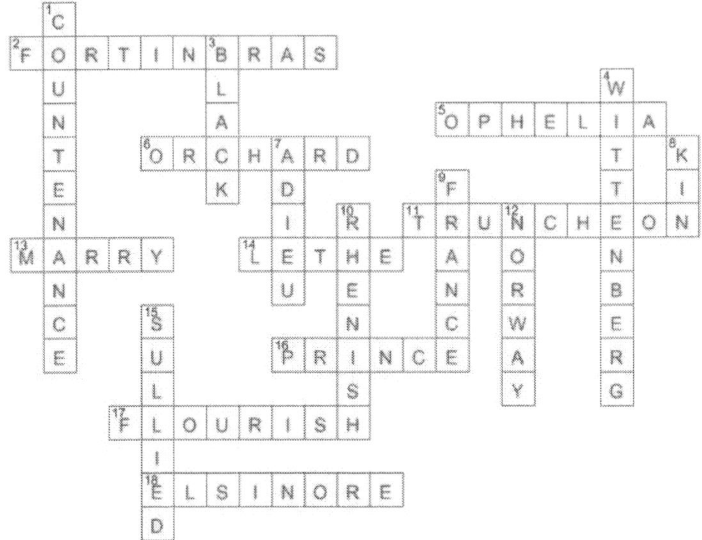

ACROSS

2. Marching against Denmark
5. Hamlet's paramour
6. Site of Old Hamlet's murder
11. Mid-sized club Ð
13. Light oath, or to wed
14. River in Hades
16. Hamlet's rank
17. Fanfare of trumpets
18. Hamlet setting

DOWN

1. "face" or "attention"
3. Hamlet's preferred color
4. Hamlet's alma mater
7. Farewell
8. "A little more than ____, and less than kind!"
9. Leartes attends school here
10. A type of wine
12. Cornelius' destination
15. "O that this too too _______ flesh would melt"

Day 1 - Vocabulary Quiz

Terms		Answers
1. ____	Assail	A. mutual ill will; hatred
2. ____	Usurp	B. attack
3. ____	Mettle	C. vague, uncertain, open to interpretation
4. ____	Portentous	D. tomb
5. ____	Dirge	E. irreligious, unholy
6. ____	Obsequious	F. like a portent; bearing an omen;
7. ____	Obstinate	foreshadowing things to come
8. ____	Impious	G. set within particular limits
9. ____	Circumscribed	H. mournful song, normally associated with
10. ____	Imminent	funerals
11. ____	Sepulcher	I. assume a position of power illegally;
12. ____	Enmity	overthrow
13. ____	Sinew	J. muscle, tissue
14. ____	Ambiguous	K. stubborn, inflexible
15. ____	Perturbed	L. disturbed, anxious
		M. related to obsequies (funerals);
		excessively obedient or servile
		N. courage; resilience
		O. unavoidable, inevitable

Vocabulary Quiz Answer Key

1. B
2. I
3. N
4. F
5. H
6. M
7. K
8. E
9. G
10. O
11. D
12. A
13. J
14. C
15. L

Day 1 - Classroom Activities

1. Good Morning, Denmark! (or, *The Elsinore Gazette*)

Kind of Activity: Collaborative Writing
Objective: Students will create a summary of a text in their own words, learn about the importance of perspective in evaluating actions and characters, and explore a play's various themes.
Common Core State Standards: CCSS.ELA-Literacy.RL.11-12.1, CCSS.ELA-Literacy.RL.11-12.3, CCSS.ELA-Literacy.RL.11-12.6
Time: 45-60 min. (You can save class time by assigning prep work for homework)

Structure:

Break students into groups of 3-6, depending on class size. Each group will produce a news broadcast covering the major events of Act I. Once the groups have been formed, students can divide the following subjects among them: National News, Foreign Affairs, and Gossip/Entertainment.

One of the aims of this activity is to make sure that students understand the action of the first act, and can describe it in their own words. That said, you should not assign specific stories, but should expect each group to cover some of the major plot points:

Old Hamlet's Death

Claudius ascension and marriage to Gertrude

Laertes' return to France

Rumors of a ghost sighting

Romance between Hamlet and Ophelia?

Fortinbras on the move

Ambassadors sent to Norway

Each broadcast should include quotes from newsmakers or "celebrities" (e.g. Hamlet, Claudius, Gertrude) and "people on the street" (Horatio, Marcellus, Bernardo). You should stipulate that these quotes should come from dialogue - not soliloquies or asides. In other words, the report should reflect events only as they would be seen by the average citizen of Denmark. The purpose of this is twofold: to help explore the play's theme of appearance vs. reality (by comparing characters' true selves to their public personae), and to demonstrate how perspective and point of view can affect the interpretation of a character.

Ideans for Differentiated Instruction: Depending on the number of extroverts or experienced actors in your class, you can have students submit this as a written group project (e.g. in the form of a paper of large poster), or have them perform an actual news broadcast.

Assessment Ideas:

Assess written reports on the basis of demonstrated understanding of the play, logical use of quotations, and accuracy of language.

If you choose to have students submit this activity as a performance, they can incorporate technology by filming their broadcast, or by incorporating different kinds of media during an in-class performance.

2. Scene Comparison

Kind of Activity: Classwide Discussion
Objective: Students will explore how staging, acting, and directing can affect the interpretation of a dramatic work.
Common Core State Standards: CCSS.ELA-Literacy.RL.11-12.7
Time: 45 min.

Structure:

Obtain copies of Kenneth Branagh's 1996 film version and the 2010 BBC/Great Performance production of *Hamlet*. Show students each version's portrayal of Act I, Scene 2, up to Hamlet's "O that this too too sullied flesh would melt" soliloquy (since it is the more "traditional" of the two, you should start with the Branagh version). As they watch, have students take notes on how each production's acting and direction affects how they interpret the scene. Here are some leading questions students can consider:

- Pay attention to the setting: How does the environment in which the scene is set affect the way you interpret the scene?

- Pay attention to the actors who are not speaking: How are they reacting to the action of the scene? How does this influence how you view certain characters?

- Pay attention to how characters speak with one another, and how the scene is blocked (that is, to the physical positioning of the characters): What do these cues reveal about the relationships between these characters?

After showing both scenes, lead a classroom discussion in which students share their observations. During this conversation, you can guide them to the following realizations:

- As it is staged in the Branagh version, scene 2 is a grand affair, while in the BBC version it is a much more intimate private gathering. This gives the scene 2 of Branagh's version the feel of a state function, as opposed to the BBC version, which feels like a family gathering.

- In the Branagh version, the characters who are not speaking are standing at full attention, giving the scene a very formal feel. In the BBC version, the characters are more relaxed. However, the fact that Polonius "lip syncs" Laertes' request to Claudius projects a much more domineering Polonius, and a much weaker and more anxious Laertes.

- The Claudius and Gertrude of Branagh's version speak to Hamlet in much gentler tones, and their proximity to him as they speak reflects more genuine affection from Claudius. Patrick Stewart's Claudius in the BBC version is a much more distant figure, standing apart from Hamlet and delivering his lines with a more critical air. What's more, the way Stewart stammers when trying to remember the name of Hamlet's school shows how removed he is from Hamlet's life.

Point out that the text for both scenes is for the most part exactly the same; it is what the director and actors bring to scene that allow for multiple interpretations.

Ideans for Differentiated Instruction: In lieu of a class-wide discussion, you can have students submit this activity as an in-class or at-home written assignment.

Assessment Ideas:

After the activity, ask each student to write a movie review in which he or she argues for one interpretation of the scene over the other. In this review, the student should evaluate as many aspects of the scene as possible: acting, direction, scenery, cinematography, costuming.

Based on their observations, students can also stage their own interpretations of the scene, incorporating technology and mixed media, if available.

Day 2 - Reading Assignment

Read Act II.

Common Core Objectives

- CCSS.ELA-Literacy.CCRA.L.4 Determine or clarify the meaning of unknown and multiple-meaning words and phrases by using context clues, analyzing meaningful word parts, and consulting general and specialized reference materials, as appropriate.
- CCSS.ELA-Literacy.CCRA.R.7 Integrate and evaluate content presented in diverse media and formats, including visually and quantitatively, as well as in words.
- CCSS.ELA-Literacy.CCRA.R.6 Assess how point of view or purpose shapes the content and style of a text.

Note that it is perfectly fine to expand any day's work into two days depending on the characteristics of the class, particularly if the class will engage in all of the suggested classroom exercises and activities and discuss all of the thought questions.

Content Summary for Teachers

Act II:

Act II opens with Polonius dispatching his servant Reynaldo to check on Laertes, who has since returned to school in Paris. He instructs Reynaldo to inquire after Laertes' behavior and reputation before meeting with him; even for this most mundane errand, Polonius recommends a course of subterfuge and intrigue. Once Reynaldo departs, Ophelia bursts in with news of a strange encounter with a disturbed and disheveled Hamlet. Polonius, believing the prince's erratic behavior to be the result Ophelia's cutting off contact with him, decides to report this matter to the king.

Claudius, meanwhile, has received good news: his diplomatic turn has succeeded in preventing war with Fortinbras, who now turns his aggression towards Denmark's other rival, Poland. That matter settled, Claudius now focuses his attention on his stepson. He has summoned Hamlet's friends Rosencrantz and Guildenstern to court, hoping they might be able to determine the cause of his distress and perhaps cheer him. Polonius, however, thinks he has already found it, and reads aloud Hamlet's love letters to Ophelia (throwing in his own literary critiques for good measure). When Polonius suggests that he "loose" his daughter upon Hamlet so that he and the king can observe their interaction in secret, Hamlet suddenly enters. After the king and queen exit, Polonius engages the prince and tries to sound his state of mind, but is thoroughly confounded by Hamlet's wit and wordplay.

After Polonius takes his leave, Rosencrantz and Guildenstern prove slightly more successful at getting Hamlet to open up about his feelings, though Hamlet rightly surmises that the pair has a hidden agenda. Hamlet muses eloquently on the depths of his melancholy, but his mood is suddenly brightened by the arrival of a company of traveling players. He entreats one of them to recite a speech recounting an episode from the fall of Troy. Moved by the player's impassioned performance, a solitary Hamlet is brought to meditate on his own predicament. How is it that someone can shed real tears over a mere fiction, while he - a prince whose father, mother, and throne have been stolen from him - can do nothing but dawdle and daydream? Inspired by the player's example, and reasoning that the ghost might be a demon out to corrupt him, Hamlet concocts a scheme to confirm his uncle's guilt: he will stage a scene that resembles his uncle's alleged murder of Old Hamlet, and present it before the whole court. If Claudius is indeed guilty, Hamlet reasons, he will no doubt see it in the king's reaction to the play.

Thought Questions (students consider while they read)

1. Pay attention to the way other characters interact with Rosencrantz and Guildenstern, and how they interact with one another. What does this tell you about Rosencrantz and Guildenstern?
2. Metatheatre is a dramatic device in which the characters in a play comment of the nature of theater itself. How does Shakespeare incorporate metatheatre in Act IV? What effect do you think this has on the audience?
3. In Hamlet's mind, Claudius is a "damned villain," but in the first two acts of the play, Claudius seems to express a genuine concern for Hamlet's well-being. How can you reconcile these diverging views of this character?
4. For someone in the midst of such a profound depression, Hamlet's mood lightens considerably with the arrival of the players. Why do you think this is so? What does it say about Hamlet's character?
5. What do we learn about the character of Fortinbras in scene 1? How does this present a contrast to the state of affairs in Denmark?

Vocabulary (in order of appearance)

Sc. i, l. 78:

- Doublet: a close-fitting men's jacket

Sc. i, l. 90:

- Perusal: examination, scrutiny, reading

Sc. ii, l. 307:

- Promontory: a elevated rock or land formation that juts out into a body of water

Sc. ii, l. 315:

- Apprehension: understanding; reason

Sc. ii, l. 325:

- Lenten: relating to Lent; spartan, meager, austere

Sc. ii, l. 346:

- Wonted: customary, usual

Sc. ii, l. 374:

- Ducat: a gold coin

Sc. ii, l. 560:

- Rogue: an unprincipled person; scoundrel

Sc. ii, l. 604:

- Malefaction: crime, misdeed

Sc. ii, l. 198:

- Slander: defamation; false statements intended to damage a person's reputation

Sc. ii, l. 309:

- Firmament: sky

Sc. ii, l. 311:

- Pestilent: toxic, deadly

Sc. ii, l. 458:

- Priam: the king of Troy in Homer's *Iliad* and Virgil's *Aeneid*

Sc. ii, l. 512:

- Hecuba: the queen of Troy in Homer's *Iliad* and Virgil's *Aeneid*

Sc. ii, l. 220:

- Tedious: dull, tiresome, boring

Additional Homework

1. A few times in Act II, Hamlet addresses Polonius as "Jephthah," who is a figure in the Old Testament's Book Of Judges. Read chapter 11 of the Book of Judges to learn more about Jephthah. Based on this reading, why do you think Hamlet refers to Polonius by this name?
2. The speech the player recites in Act II is adapted from Book II of Virgil's *Aeneid*, which details the fall of Troy in its second chapter. Read Book II, lines 530-563 of the *Aeneid*, and compare this version to Shakespeare's adaption. Why do you think Shakespeare chose this specific scene? What does it have to say about the nature of revenge?

Day 2 - Discussion of Thought Questions

1. Pay attention to the way other characters interact with Rosencrantz and Guildenstern, and how they interact with one another. What does this tell you about Rosencrantz and Guildenstern?

   Time: 5 min.

   Discussion: At the beginning of scene 2, when the reader is introduced to the pair, Claudius addresses them as "Rosencrantz and gentle Guildenstern," and immediately after, Gertrude refers to them as "Guildenstern and gentle Rosencrantz." Right from the start, then, the audience is given the impression that the characters are interchangeable. Unlike fully formed characters such as Hamlet, Claudius, and Polonius, Rosencrantz and Guildenstern seem to have no distinguishing characterstics. As an exercise, have your students switch the lines between Rosencrantz and Guildenstern in Scene 2 - does this have any discernible effect on the action of the scene? Rosencrantz and Guildenstern thus have no real identities of their own, they are just instruments used by the scheming Claudius.

2. Metatheatre is a dramatic device in which the characters in a play comment of the nature of theater itself. How does Shakespeare incorporate metatheatre in Act IV? What effect do you think this has on the audience?

   Time: 5 min.

   Discussion: Shakespeare incorporates metatheatre in Hamlet's soliloquy at the end of Act II. What is most interesting about this scene is that while the *character* of Hamlet marvels at the player's ability to conjure up real emotions over a situation that is entirely fictional, the *actor* who is on stage playing Hamlet is essentially doing the same thing. This draws the audience further into the action of the play because it makes Hamlet almost a member of the audience (that is, he is also viewing a dramatic performance), while at the same time increasing the audience's empathy for his character.

3. In Hamlet's mind, Claudius is a "damned villain," but in the first two acts of the play, Claudius seems to express a genuine concern for Hamlet's well-being. How can you reconcile these diverging views of this character?

   Time: 5 min.

   Discussion: Responses for this question may vary. Villain though he may be, Claudius' affection for Gertrude seems sincere, so it could be that his concern for Hamlet's state of mind may be an extension of his own love for Gertrude. On the other hand, it is also possible that this "concern" might just be another example of Claudius' deceitfulness - after all, focusing the court's attention on Hamlet's distress is a convenient distraction from the suspicious circumstances surrounding Old Hamlet's death.

4. For someone in the midst of such a profound depression, Hamlet's mood lightens considerably with the arrival of the players. Why do you think this is so? What does it say about Hamlet's character?

   Time: 5 min.

   Discussion: Responses will vary. It is possible that Hamlet's mood brightens with the arrival of the players because in many ways, Hamlet is himself an actor. But more than that, Hamlet is a character who often lives in a world of his own imagination, similar to the world of imagination the players inhabit when they take the stage.

5. What do we learn about the character of Fortinbras in scene 1? How does this present a contrast to the state of affairs in Denmark?

   Time: 5 min.

   Discussion: In this scene, we learn that after a visit from Claudius' ambassadors, the king of Norway has reprimanded his nephew Fortinbras for his aggressive stance against Denmark. Fortinbras accepts this rebuke, and is rewarded by his uncle with a commission to attack Poland. This shows that, moreso than Hamlet, Fortinbras is a man who is able to accept the reality of his situation. Whereas Hamlet is a character of thought and deliberation, Fortinbras is a character of action.

Day 2 - Short Answer Quiz

1. What errand does Polonius give Reynaldo?

___

2. What does Ophelia reveal to Polonius in Scene 1?

___

3. What does Polonius believe to be the cause of Hamlet's madness?

___

4. What errand does Claudius give Rosencrantz and Guildenstern?

___

5. How do Rosencrantz and Guildenstern know Hamlet?

___

6. What news does Voltemand bring from Norway?

___

7. Whose arrival interrupts the conversation between Hamlet, Rosencrantz, and Guildenstern?

8. What secret does Hamlet get Rosencrantz and Guildenstern to reveal?

9. What scene does Hamlet ask one of the players to recite?

10. How does Hamlet play to use the players in his revenge against Claudius?

Short Answer Quiz Key

1. To check in on Laertes while he is away at school in Paris.
2. Ophelia reveals that Hamlet came to her chamber, acting strangely and looking disoriented and disheveled.
3. His love for Ophelia.
4. To find the cause of Hamlet's sullen behavior.
5. They are his childhood friends and fellow classmates at the University of Wittenberg.
6. The king of Norway has chastised his nephew Fortinbras for threatening war against Denmark. After this rebuke, Fortinbras turns his army against Poland instead.
7. The players.
8. That they have been sent by the king.
9. The murder of King Priam of Troy by Achilles' son Pyrrhus. ("A scene from the Trojan war" or "a scene from Greek mythology" would also be acceptable.)
10. By having them stage a play he has rewritten, one that includes a scene that is similar to Claudius' murder of Old Hamlet.

Day 2 - Crossword Puzzle

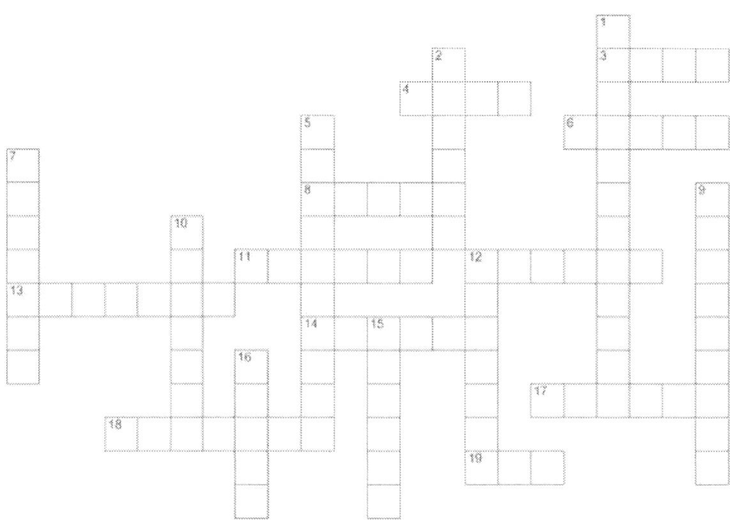

ACROSS

3. Used to "catch the conscience of the king"
4. Prefer, dersire (archaic)
6. Curtain
8. Lord, master
11. Usual; out of habit
12. Fortinbras' new target
13. Ophelia returned these to Hamlet
14. The player sheds tears for her
17. Roman dramatist
18. The "soul of wit"
19. Reynaldo's mission in France

DOWN

1. Understanding
2. Type of sword
5. Depression
7. Short jacket
9. Returns from Norway
10. Personification of fate or luck
12. Writer of Roman comedies
15. Small room
16. King of Troy

Crossword Puzzle Answer Key

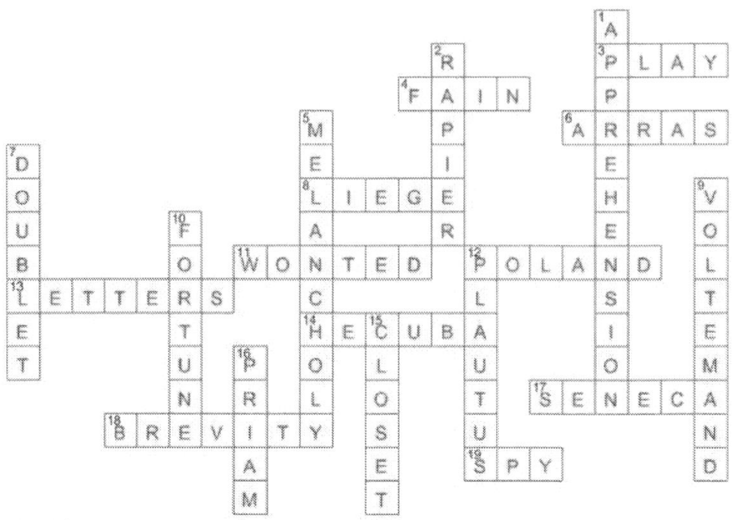

ACROSS

3. Used to "catch the conscience of the king"
4. Prefer, dersire (archaic)
6. Curtain
8. Lord, master
11. Usual; out of habit
12. Fortinbras' new target
13. Ophelia returned these to Hamlet
14. The player sheds tears for her
17. Roman dramatist
18. The "soul of wit"
19. Reynaldo's mission in France

DOWN

1. Understanding
2. Type of sword
5. Depression
7. Short jacket
9. Returns from Norway
10. Personification of fate or luck
12. Writer of Roman comedies
15. Small room
16. King of Troy

Day 2 - Vocabulary Quiz

Terms

1. ____ Doublet
2. ____ Perusal
3. ____ Promontory
4. ____ Apprehension
5. ____ Lenten
6. ____ Wonted
7. ____ Ducat
8. ____ Rogue
9. ____ Malefaction
10. ____ Slander
11. ____ Firmament
12. ____ Pestilent
13. ____ Priam
14. ____ Hecuba
15. ____ Tedious

Answers

A. a elevated rock or land formation that juts out into a body of water
B. the king of Troy in Homer's Iliad and Virgil's Aeneid
C. crime, misdeed
D. an unprincipled person; scoundrel
E. dull, tiresome, boring
F. customary, usual
G. a gold coin
H. sky
I. examination, scrutiny, reading
J. relating to Lent; spartan, meager, austere
K. toxic, deadly
L. the queen of Troy in Homer's Iliad and Virgil's Aeneid
M. defamation; false statements intended to damage a person's reputation
N. a close-fitting men's jacket
O. understanding; reason

Vocabulary Quiz Answer Key

1. N
2. I
3. A
4. O
5. J
6. F
7. G
8. D
9. C
10. M
11. H
12. K
13. B
14. L
15. E

Day 2 - Classroom Activities

1. Hamlet's Madness on Stage and Screen

 Kind of Activity: Mixed Media
 Objective: Students will explore how differences in media can affect how a literary work is interpreted.
 Common Core State Standards: CCSS.ELA-Literacy.RL.11-12.7
 Time: 30-45 min.

 Structure:

 Obtain a copy of Laurence Olivier's 1948 film version of *Hamlet.* Show students the interaction between Olivier's Hamlet and Felix Aylmer's Polonius in Act II, Scene 2. As before, have students take notes on how the staging, acting, etc. affect the way they feel about the scene. Lead a short discussion in which you ask students about their reaction to that scene. Then, show students the same scene from John Gielgud's 1964 Broadway production, starring Richard Burton as Hamlet and Hume Cronyn as Polonius. (Available online at http://www.youtube.com/watch?v=l93LR6Sw75Q) Have students take notes about how their reaction to this stage version differed from their reaction to the film version.

 Lead a classroom discussion in which students explore the differences between these two portrayals. Stress that one of the main differences is that one is a film, while the other is a play staged before a live audience. How do these differences in media affect our reaction to the scene?

 Here are some other leading questions you can ask to move the discussion along:

 What perspective are we given when watching these characters interact? How do the actors in each version physically interact with one another? How does this affect your interpretation of the relationship between their characters?

 How do the sets and costumes affect your response to the scene?

 How did the presence of a live audience in the stage version affect your interpretation of the scene?

 At some point in the discussion, introduce the concept of the fourth wall in drama, by pointing out how Hume Cronyn uses it to great effect. How does his "breaking" this fourth wall affect the mood of this scene?

Student responses will vary, but you can guide students to the realization that the traditional setting and formal direction of the Olivier version portray Hamlet's madness as unsettling, while the unconventional staging and more natural performances in the stage version make the scene much more humorous and playful. You should stress while these interpretations are completely different, the text of each scene is exactly the same. The stark differences between the two demonstrate how much presentation affects our interprctation of a dramatic work.

Ideans for Differentiated Instruction: In lieu of a class-wide discussion, you can have students submit this activity as an in-class or at-home written assignment.

Assessment Ideas:
If the technology is available, have students film their own interpretations of this scene. Encourage them to be creative, use unconventional staging, costuming, props, or direction to create a new take on this scene.

2. Hamlet's Sense of Humor

Kind of Activity: Collaborative Writing
Objective: Students will analyze how the difference between the literal and intended meanings of words and phrases can affect the humor of a text
Common Core State Standards: CCSS.ELA-Literacy.RL.11-12.6, CCSS.ELA-Literacy.L.11-12.4
Time: 15-20 min.

Structure: Break students into pairs or small groups and have them analyze Hamlet's dialogue with Polonius in Act II, Scene 2. In particular, students should identify instances in which Hamlet uses words or phrases with double meanings. Have each pair or group create a chart that compares the literal meaning of Hamlet's speech with his intended meaning. Student responses will vary, but should focus on at least some of the following terms: "fishmonger," "conception," "matter," "slander," "walk out of the air," "take my leave," etc.

Ideans for Differentiated Instruction: For students who made be struggling with the material, you may want to go through the text with them to identify the targeted words first, then have them consult reference materials to determine how these words can have multiple meanings.

Assessment Ideas:

Ask students to identify more contemporary examples of wordplay and double meanings in a contemporary comedy or drama.

Give students a brief creative writing assignment in which they write a dialogue that makes use of puns and double entendres.

Day 3 - Reading Assignment

Read Act III.

Common Core Objectives

- CCSS.ELA-Literacy.CCRA.R.1 Read closely to determine what the text says explicitly and to make logical inferences from it; cite specific textual evidence when writing or speaking to support conclusions drawn from the text.
- CCSS.ELA-Literacy.CCRA.W.1 Write arguments to support claims in an analysis of substantive topics or texts using valid reasoning and relevant and sufficient evidence.
- CCSS.ELA-Literacy.CCRA.SL.4 Present information, findings, and supporting evidence such that listeners can follow the line of reasoning and the organization, development, and style are appropriate to task, purpose, and audience.
- CCSS.ELA-Literacy.CCRA.SL.1 Prepare for and participate effectively in a range of conversations and collaborations with diverse partners, building on others' ideas and expressing their own clearly and persuasively.
- CCSS.ELA-Literacy.CCRA.R.7 Integrate and evaluate content presented in diverse media and formats, including visually and quantitatively, as well as in words.

Note that it is perfectly fine to expand any day's work into two days depending on the characteristics of the class, particularly if the class will engage in all of the suggested classroom exercises and activities and discuss all of the thought questions.

Content Summary for Teachers

Act III:

Rosencrantz and Guildenstern open Act III with their report to Claudius and Gertrude: Hamlet is indeed depressed, but the prospect of presenting a play before the king and queen has improved his mood greatly. This pleases the king, who then asks the queen to take her leave, so that he and Polonius can carry out their plan to spy on Ophelia and Hamlet. Polonius directs Ophelia to take her place as he and Claudius hide behind an arras.

Hamlet then enters and delivers his soliloquy on the mystery of being and death. He breaks off when Ophelia enters, ostensibly to return certain tokens the prince had given her. After a somewhat awkward exchange, Hamlet suddenly turns on Ophelia, renouncing his love for her and railing against the dishonesty of women. He storms off, and Ophelia collapses in misery and self-reproach. Polonius feels this behavior confirms his earlier suspicions, but to Claudius, it points to a deeper, darker secret.

The next scene begins with a flurry of text, as Hamlet rattles off a series of instructions to his players. Horatio enters, and after paying a touching tribute to him, Hamlet informs him of his plan for the evening. As the royal entourage enters, Hamlet adopts his antic disposition, mocking Polonius and lewdly flirting with Ophelia. After a short pantomime scene, the play begins. A player king and queen exchange loving vows before the king retires for a nap. Then, just as the ghost described, a villain enters and pours poison into the king's ear, killing him. As Hamlet predicted, Claudius is greatly affected by this scene, and his outburst brings the play to an abrupt end. Hamlet openly rejoices over this, seeing it as a confirmation of the ghost's tale. Gertrude, however, is not amused, and summons Hamlet to her chamber to voice her displeasure.

Claudius, meanwhile, has resolved to send Hamlet away to England, and instructs Rosencrantz and Guildenstern to prepare for the voyage. Left alone, Claudius repents his crimes, but realizes that he can never find absolution unless he renounces all he has gained from his brother's murder. Knowing this can never be, Claudius kneels in a pitiful attempt at prayer. Hamlet, finding Claudius thus unguarded, moves to kill him on the spot. However, his hand is stayed by the realization that killing Claudius while he is at prayer will probably send him to heaven, sparing him the daily torture that his father must endure. He resolves to find a more opportune moment, perhaps when Claudius is in the midst of some wickedness.

In Gertrude's chamber, Polonius advises Gertrude to be firm with her son, then hides behind a curtain to monitor the proceedings. Hamlet bursts in, and his menacing behavior so frightens Gertrude that Polonius cries out for help. Hamlet, thinking the person hiding might be Claudius, stabs through the curtain, killing Polonius. His mistake realized, Hamlet regrets the old man's death, but continues to lash out at his mother. At the height of his tirade, the ghost intervenes, reminding Hamlet of his duty, both to murder his uncle and to comfort his mother. For some reason, Gertrude is unable to see the ghost, and is startled by Hamlet's seeming madness. Hamlet, steadying himself, reassures Gertrude that his madness is but a cover. He urges her to reject any further advances from Claudius, and to tell no one what he has revealed. She agrees, and Hamlet withdraws, dragging the body of Polonius with him.

Thought Questions (students consider while they read)

1. Suppose that Hamlet is aware that Claudius and Polonius are spying on him in scene 1. How might this affect your reading of the "To be or not to be" speech?
2. How does the appearance of the ghost in Act I affect Hamlet's decision-making in Act III, Scene 3?
3. How do Hamlet's actions in Act 3 strengthen or weaken the claim that he is indecisive?

4. Compare Hamlet's conversation with Ophelia in Act III, Scene 1 to his soliloquy in Act I, Scene 2 (129-158). What themes do they have in common? What can you infer about Hamlet's treatment of Ophelia?
5. How do both Hamlet and Polonius act as "directors" in *Hamlet*? How might these similarities be seen as a commentary on theater vs. reality?

Vocabulary (in order of appearance)

Sc. i, l.22:

- Entreat: to implore, beseech

Sc. i, l.33:

- Bestow: to place, put away

Sc. i, l. 36:

- Affliction: malady, source of pain or anguish

Sc. i, l. 47:

- Visage: face

Sc. i, l. 84:

- Hue: color, tint

Sc. i, l. 89:

- Nymph: fairy, goddess

Sc. 2, l. 10:

- Tatters: shreds, rags

Sc. 2, l. 204:

- Revel: carouse, have fun

Sc. 2, l. 302:

- Vouchsafe: give, offer, grant

Sc. 3, l. 25:

- Fetters: chains, shackles, restraints

Sc. 3, l. 28:

- Arras: curtain, tapestry

Sc. 3, l. 58:

- Gilded: covered with a thin layer of gold

Sc. 4, l. 12:

- Idle: foolish

Sc. 4, l. 101:

- Diadem: crown; symbol of royalty or sovereignty

Sc. 4, l. 119:

- Discourse: conversation, communication, intellectual exchange

Sc. 4, l. 216:

- Prating: verbose, overly talkative

Additional Homework

1. In Acts II and III, Hamlet and his companions make several references to Fortune with a capital "F" - that is, they saw Fortune less as the sum of one's circumstances or mere blind luck, but as an active, almost sentient force in people's lives. The way people's lives are shaped by Fortune is a recurring theme in Shakespeare's plays. Do some research on the importance of Fortune to Renaissance minds. Why do you think they developed this conceit?

Day 3 - Discussion of Thought Questions

1. Suppose that Hamlet is aware that Claudius and Polonius are spying on him in scene 1. How might this affect your reading of the "To be or not to be" speech?

   Time: 5-10 min.

   Discussion: If Hamlet believes that he is alone, then we can interpret his "To be or not to be" speech to be a sincere mediation on the nature of life and death. However, if he is aware of Claudius and Polonius' presence, then it's possible that this speech is just another red herring designed to further convince them of his madness. And if it is so, this would also lead the reader to question the seriousness of Hamlet's contemplation of suicide.

2. How does the appearance of the ghost in Act I affect Hamlet's decision-making in Act III, Scene 3?

   Time: 5 minutes

   Discussion: In Act I, the ghost tells Hamlet that since he was murdered before doing penance for his sins, he must spend his days in fiery torment to atone for them. With this system of divine retribution in mind, Hamlet reasons that killing Claudius while he is repenting his sins will send Claudius to heaven, thus sparing him the punishment his father must undergo. As a result, Hamlet declines what is a golden opportunity to take his revenge against his uncle.

3. How do Hamlet's actions in Act 3 strengthen or weaken the claim that he is indecisive?

   Time: 5-10 min.

   Discussion: Answers for this question will vary. The central device of Act III - the play within a play - can itself be seen as an instrument of Hamlet's delay, since it only postpones what he already knows he must do. Hamlet's failure to take advantage of his opportunity to kill Claudius at prayer in Act III could be read as further evidence of this indecisiveness. He shows no such hesitation in the next scene, however, when he recklessly murders Polonius, mistaking him for Claudius. In this light, Hamlet's decision not to kill Claudius at prayer can be seen as prudence, not a lack of resolution. After all, since Hamlet now knows that what the ghost is said is true, that means the vision of the afterlife he described is true as well. In this context, Hamlet's decision makes sense - he must find an opportunity not only to punish Claudius's body, but his spirit as well.

4. Compare Hamlet's conversation with Ophelia in Act III, Scene 1 to his soliloquy in Act I, Scene 2 (129-158). What themes do they have in common? What can you infer about Hamlet's treatment of Ophelia?

   Time: 5-10 min.

   Discussion: In both his soliloquy and his conversation with Ophelia, Hamlet expresses his view that all women are ultimately "frail" and faithless, a view that stems from his anger and disappointment over his mother's marriage to Claudius (an act that, in Hamlet's view, makes her unfaithful to his father). In lashing out at Ophelia, then, it could be said that Hamlet is in fact lashing out at his own mother. What undermines Hamlet's view, and makes his attack all the more unfair, is the character of Ophelia herself, who is genuinely devoted to her father, brother, and ultimately, to Hamlet himself.

5. How do both Hamlet and Polonius act as "directors" in *Hamlet*? How might these similarities be seen as a commentary on theater vs. reality?

   Time: 5-10 min.

   Discussion: While Hamlet directs the players in a more literal sense, Polonius is a "director" in his own right, often setting up "performances" designed to glean important information or provoke a particular emotional response in his subjects. This contrast shows that while there is a certain element of reality in theater, there is also a certain element of theatricality in everyday life.

Day 3 - Short Answer Quiz

1. What other subject of a Shakespeare play does Polonius reference in Act III?

2. According to his conversation with Ophelia, what institution would Hamlet like to see abolished?

3. What errand does Claudius plan to give Hamlet in order to get him out of Denmark?

4. What does Hamlet admire most about Horatio?

5. How does Hamlet's treatment of Ophelia differ from scene 1 to scene 2?

6. How would you describe Hamlet's mood after the play?

7. What is Claudius doing in scene 3 that prevents Hamlet from killing him?

8. Who does Hamlet kill in Gertrude's chamber?

9. Who does Hamlet *think* he has killed?

10. What is Hamlet able to see that his mother cannot?

Short Answer Quiz Key

1. Julius Caesar.
2. Marriage.
3. Claudius plans to send Hamlet to England to collect overdue tribute from its king.
4. His stoicism; that is, his ability to accept good or bad fortune with a steady attitude.
5. In scene 1, Hamlet is very cruel to Ophelia; in scene 2, he seems to be flirting with her.
6. A few answers are acceptable here: joyous, boastful, triumphant, etc.
7. Praying.
8. Polonius.
9. Claudius.
10. The ghost.

Day 3 - Crossword Puzzle

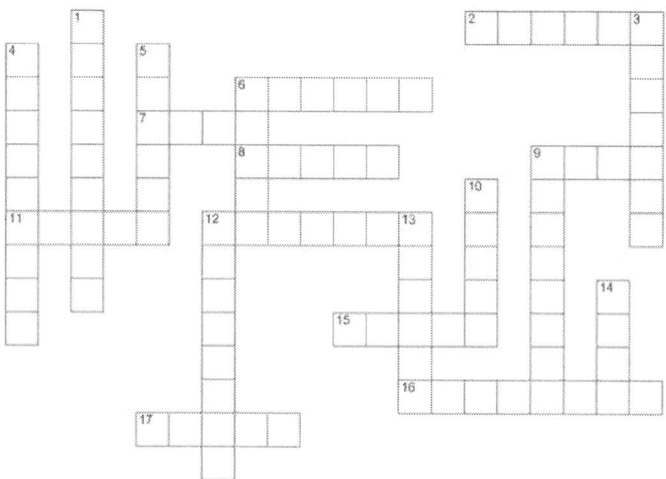

ACROSS

2. dagger
6. crown
7. foolish, or inactive
8. to attempt
9. according to Hamlet, playing this is "as easy as lying"
11. in two
12. "_______'s cart"; sun
15. interrupts Hamlet's condemnation of Gertrude
16. pantomime
17. _____ to be kind

DOWN

1. give or grant
3. Ophelia should go here, according to Hamlet
4. title of Hamlet's play
5. prayers
6. the "undiscovered country"
9. killed by accident
10. coin
12. precedes the action of a play
13. exclamation, short for "God's blood"
14. emperor who murdered his mother

Crossword Puzzle Answer Key

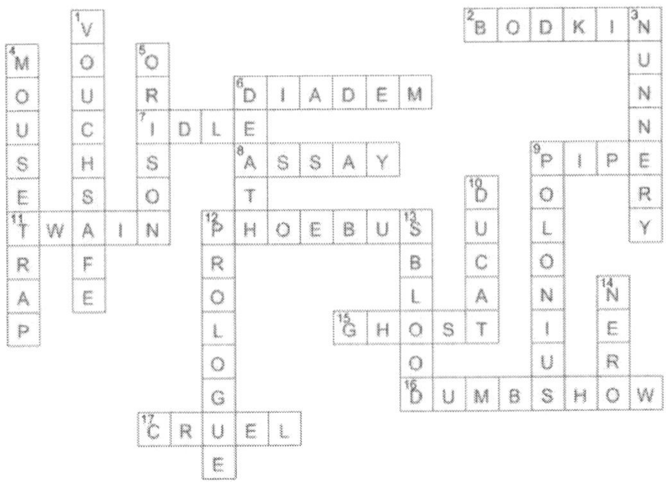

ACROSS

2. dagger
6. crown
7. foolish, or inactive
8. to attempt
9. according to Hamlet, playing this is "as easy as lying"
11. in two
12. "_______'s cart"; sun
15. interrupts Hamlet's condemnation of Gertrude
16. pantomime
17. ______ to be kind

DOWN

1. give or grant
3. Ophelia should go here, according to Hamlet
4. title of Hamlet's play
5. prayers
6. the "undiscovered country"
9. killed by accident
10. coin
12. precedes the action of a play
13. exclamation, short for "God's blood"
14. emperor who murdered his mother

Day 3 - Vocabulary Quiz

Terms	Answers
1. ____ Entreat	A. curtain, tapestry
2. ____ Bestow	B. covered with a thin layer of gold
3. ____ Affliction	C. malady, source of pain or anguish
4. ____ Visage	D. fairy, goddess
5. ____ Hue	E. give, offer, grant
6. ____ Nymph	F. to implore, beseech
7. ____ Tatters	G. carouse, have fun
8. ____ Revel	H. shreds, rags
9. ____ Vouchsafe	I. to place, put away
10. ____ Fetters	J. conversation, communication, intellectual exchange
11. ____ Arras	K. chains, shackles, restraints
12. ____ Gilded	L. verbose, overly talkative
13. ____ Idle	M. foolish
14. ____ Diadem	N. crown; symbol of royalty or sovereignty
15. ____ Discourse	O. color, tint
16. ____ Prating	P. face

Vocabulary Quiz Answer Key

1. F
2. I
3. C
4. P
5. O
6. D
7. H
8. G
9. E
10. K
11. A
12. B
13. M
14. N
15. J
16. L

Day 3 - Classroom Activities

1. Gertrude on Trial

Kind of Activity: Group Work
Objective: Students will present and defend an argument based on a close reading of the text.
Common Core State Standards: CCSS.ELA-Literacy.SL.11-12.4, CCSS.ELA-Literacy.W.11-12.1a, CCSS.ELA-Literacy.RL.11-12.1
Time: 30-60 min.

Structure:

Is Gertrude a villain or heroine? Over the years, scholars have debated her role in the play: Were she and Claudius having an affair before Old Hamlet's death? If so, was she complicit in Old Hamlet's murder? Or is she just another innocent victim of Claudius' crimes?

Since Gertrude is not afforded an extended soliloquy along the lines of Hamlet's or Claudius' (or even an aside, for that matter), we know relatively little about her motivations, or her innermost feelings about the events surrounding her. We can, however, form conjectures based on the clues we are given throughout the text.

In this activity, students will put the character of Gertrude on "trial" for the murder of Old Hamlet. Divide your class into two teams - Defense and Prosecution - and give them time to gather their "evidence" from the text (you can assign this task for homework, if you like). Depending on the size of the class and the time or space allowed, you can have each group elect representatives to give oral arguments, or you can just have students submit written arguments.

You should assign students to their teams; students should NOT be able to pick their own. This is not only to ensure that each side will have a relatively equal number of students, but also to give students the challenge of researching and defending arguments and opinions that might not necessarily be their own.

Answers will, of course vary. Students on the side of the Prosecution might point to Hamlet's rage as evidence of his mother's obvious guilt, or the ghost's reference to her as a "seeming virtuous queen". Students on the side of the Defense might counter by citing Gertrude's genuine devotion to her son, or the fact that Claudius does not include her in any of his other schemes. Whatever the case, students must back up their arguments with direct quotes from the text. If the technology is available, students can also submit clips from different film versions that seem to point to a particular interpretation of Gertrude's role. If any of your students have acting experience, you can encourage them to stage relevant scenes and submit them as evidence.

Ideans for Differentiated Instruction: If students are struggling to interpret Gertrude as either guilty or not guilty, lead the class through a discussion in which everyone brainstorms evidence for both sides of the argument. Then have students structure their arguments in groups, using the discussion as a basis.

Assessment Ideas:
As the activity indicates, Gertrude never delivers a soliloquy in *Hamlet*. Building on their own interpretations of the text, have students write a soliloquy for Gertrude that discusses her role in / reaction to Old Hamlet's death, and her reasons for marrying Claudius.

2. The Pantomime Scene

Kind of Activity: Role Play
Objective: Students will examine how movements, gestures, and facial expressions can convey or enhance a message.
Common Core State Standards: CCSS.ELA-Literacy.SL.11-12.1, CCSS.ELA-Literacy.RL.11-12.7
Time: 60 min. (May take more than one classroom session - you might want to assign prep work for homework.)

Structure:

This exercise is based on the short "dumb show" that precedes the play-within-a-play in Act III, Scene 2. Its purpose is to allow students to explore the ways drama give characters the space to communicate through nonverbal cues such as gestures, facial expressions, and physical interaction.

Divide the class into smaller groups (the size of each group will depend on the the size of the class, and the scenes you choose for them). Select different scenes from Acts I-III (try to avoid scenes with extended monologues), and assign one scene to each group. The goal of each group will be to convey the action and meaning of its assigned scene only through movement, gestures, and facial expressions.

If you have any experienced actors or extroverts in your class, try to disperse them among the different groups. You can assign specific roles if you wish, or have students work out the casting among themselves. Depending on the makeup of your class, you should expect to have girls performing male roles, given the small number of female characters in *Hamlet*.

Once the roles have been assigned, have each student sketch a short bio of their character based on the information given in the text (you can also encourage your students to be a bit more creative and "invent" biographical details, so long as they have some logical grounding in the text). When staging their scene, students should use these sketches to help them answer questions such as:

How would my character stand or walk?

How would my character physically interact with other characters?

When delivering certain lines, what gestures or facial expressions would my character use?

When not speaking, how would my character react to the action of a scene?

If you like, you can present this activity as a sort of "game" in which the other groups have to try to guess what scene is being presented, and offer some sort of prize for the most convincing portrayal. Such an incentive will help motivate students to make sure their staging stays true to the text, and discourage clowning or overacting. After the other group have offered their guesses, you can have the presenting group reveal the scene, and briefly explain their characterization choices.

Ideans for Differentiated Instruction: For students who are uncomfortable with performing or who prefer to work independently, you can assign this activity as a written assignment in which students have to imagine themselves as directors, and write a series of "notes" for each of the actors in a given scene.

Assessment Ideas:
If you would like to add a written component to this activity, have students take notes in which they answer the leading questions given in the activity, and elaborate on their non-verbal approach to their assigned characters.

Day 4 - Reading Assignment

Read Act IV.

Common Core Objectives

- CCSS.ELA-Literacy.CCRA.R.6 Assess how point of view or purpose shapes the content and style of a text.
- CCSS.ELA-Literacy.CCRA.R.1 Read closely to determine what the text says explicitly and to make logical inferences from it; cite specific textual evidence when writing or speaking to support conclusions drawn from the text.

Note that it is perfectly fine to expand any day's work into two days depending on the characteristics of the class, particularly if the class will engage in all of the suggested classroom exercises and activities and discuss all of the thought questions.

Content Summary for Teachers

Act IV:

Act IV picks up immediately where Act III left off. Gertrude reveals to Claudius that Hamlet, in his madness, has murdered Polonius. Realizing that he was the intended victim, Claudius orders Rosencrantz and Guildenstern to seek out Hamlet and recover Polonius' body. The pair soon finds Hamlet and implores him to tell them where the corpse is hidden, but the inscrutable prince leads them on a wild goose chase instead.

When Hamlet is at last brought before the king, he is defiant, but is soon made to reveal that he has hidden Polonius' body in the lobby. Claudius orders his attendants to retrieve it, and informs Hamlet that, for his own safety, he must be sent away to England. Hamlet relents, but openly mocks the king as he departs. Claudius, left alone, prepares a letter for the English king, commanding him to kill Hamlet upon his arrival.

The next scene opens on a plain in Denmark, where Fortinbras' army is seeking safe passage for its campaign against Poland. Hamlet, on his way to England, approaches one of Fortinbras' captains and learns from him that the army's target is a small, worthless patch of land. Nevertheless, it is already well defended by the Polish army, and taking it will no doubt cost thousands of lives. The sight of so many men marching to their deaths for a cause as flimsy as "honor" amazes Hamlet; in another memorable soliloquy, he resolves (yet again) to cast off his philosophizing, and renews his vows of revenge.

Back at the palace, Ophelia, her mind completely overthrown, seeks out an audience with a reluctant queen. Her speech is mostly nonsensical, interspersed with bits from nursery rhymes and bawdy songs, but it is obvious that she has been driven mad by her father's murder and Hamlet's cruelty. Claudius is deeply moved by the pitiful scene, but must turn his attention to a new problem: Laertes, quickly returned from France, has broken into the palace at the head of a large mob, demanding satisfaction for his father's death and secret burial. As Claudius proclaims his innocence, Ophelia re-enters, and Laertes is subdued by his grief and pity over her condition. Claudius comforts Laertes, and leads him away so they can discuss the circumstances surrounding his father's death.

In another part of the castle, Horatio receives an extraordinary letter from Hamlet: en route to England, his ship was attacked by pirates. During the ensuing battle, Hamlet boarded the pirate vessel, but was taken prisoner once the two ships were separated. In a separate letter to Claudius, Hamlet announces his imminent return. Startled at this turn of events, Claudius hatches a new scheme: circulating stories of Laertes' superior skill, Claudius will set a wager on a fencing match between Laertes and Hamlet. Claudius is convinced that Hamlet's vanity will force him to accept the challenge, and at the duel, he plans to switch Laertes' foil with a sharpened, poisoned sword that will ensure Hamlet's death with just one blow. To secure the matter further, Claudius will offer Hamlet a poisoned chalice during the bout. Any satisfaction Claudius and Laertes might have derived from the plan is immediately dashed by the news of Ophelia's mysterious death by drowning. This grief upon grief is almost too much for Laertes to bear as he exits, followed by a beleaguered Claudius and Gertrude.

Thought Questions (students consider while they read)

1. How would you characterize Hamlet's reaction to Polonius' death?
2. How is Laertes' predicament similar to Hamlet's? How are the two characters different from one another?
3. How is Claudius able to persuade Laertes to agree to duel Hamlet in scene 5? How does this relate to Hamlet's soliloquy in scene 4?
4. Consider the songs Ophelia sings in scene 5. What might these songs have to say about her relationship with Hamlet?
5. How are Hamlet and Fortinbras similar? How are they different?

Vocabulary (in order of appearance)

Sc. i, l. 23:

- Pith: innermost core; essence

Sc. i, l. 32:

- Countenance: admit; tolerate

Sc. ii, l. 6:

- Compound (v): mix; combine to form a whole.

Sc. iii, l. 20:

- Convocation: gathering

Sc. iii, l. 44:

- Bark: ship; vessel

Sc. iv, l. 24:

- Garrison: position or entrench troops

Sc. iv, l. 40:

- Craven: cowardly

Sc. v, l. 2:

- Importunate: persistent; unyielding

Sc. v, l. 15:

- Conjecture: assumption; speculation

Sc. v, l. 96:

- Superfluous: extra; more than what is necessary

Sc. v, l. 102:

- Rabble: angry, disorderly mob

Sc. v, l. 211:

- Obscure: hidden; concealed

Sc. vii, l. 79:

- Livery: costume; uniform

Sc. vii, l. 136:

- Foil: thin sword used in fencing

Sc. vii, l. 190:

- Fain: willingly, eagerly

Additional Homework

1. Research the role of pirates in the expansion of English sea power during the sixteenth century. In Act IV, Hamlet refers to his pirate captors as "thieves of mercy." How would this morally ambiguous description make sense to an Elizabethan audience?

Day 4 - Discussion of Thoughtful Questions

1. How would you characterize Hamlet's reaction to Polonius' death?

   Time: 5 min.

   Discussion: For someone as sensitive and contemplative as Hamlet, his reaction to his killing of Polonius is remarkably cavalier. This could, of course, be a part of his "antic disposition", though Hamlet's previous interactions with Polonius revealed that he had little regard for the "tedious old fool".

2. How is Laertes' predicament similar to Hamlet's? How are the two characters different from one another?

   Time: 5 min.

   Discussion: Like Hamlet, Laertes is the son of a murdered father who dies in obscurity. However, unlike Hamlet, who obsesses over the right approach to his revenge, Laertes dives headlong into it, rushing back from Paris to storm Elsinore and demand satisfaction. Laertes' approach to his revenge might be more emotional satisfying on a superficial level, but since he must ally himself to the devious Claudius to get it, it is far less satisfying morally.

3. How is Claudius able to persuade Laertes to agree to duel Hamlet in scene 5? How does this relate to Hamlet's soliloquy in scene 4?

   Time: 5 min.

   Discussion:

   Claudius is able to persuade Laertes to agree to duel Hamlet much in the same way he plans to convince Hamlet to duel - by appealing to his vanity and sense of honor. This appeal to harkens back to Hamlet's soliloquy at the end of scene 4, in which he observes that:

Rightly to be great

Is not to stir without great argument,

But greatly to find quarrel in a straw

When honour's at the stake.

4. Consider the songs Ophelia sings in scene 5. What might these songs have to say about her relationship with Hamlet?

   Time: 5 min.

   Discussion: Aside from the songs that directly touch upon her father's death, the other songs Ophelia sings deal with a lover wooing a maiden with vows of love, only to jilt her in the end. The overt sexual content of these songs point to a sexual relationship between Hamlet and Ophelia, and demonstrate that his repudiation of her love is one of the causes of her mental collapse.

5. How are Hamlet and Fortinbras similar? How are they different?

   Time: 5 min.

   Discussion: Like Laertes, Fortinbras stands as a dramatic counterpart to Hamlet, in that he is also a son seeking revenge for his father's murder. Unlike Hamlet, who rages against his fate and loses himself in introspection, Fortinbras seems to be a man who is able to accept the reality of his situation, and when his attempt at revenge is thwarted, he finds other outlets for his aggression. While this might seem commendable on the surface, Hamlet himself reminds us that Fortinbras' efforts come at the expense of the thousands of innocent lives that will be lost in his military campaigns.

Day 4 - Short Answer Quiz

1. What has Hamlet hidden at the beginning of this scene?

____

2. What does Claudius ask of the King of England?

____

3. What does Hamlet encounter before leaving for England?

____

4. What effect does Polonius' death have on Ophelia?

____

5. What is Laertes' reaction to Polonius' death?

____

6. What happens to Hamlet during his voyage to England?

____

7. What is Fortinbras' army fighting for?

____

8. With what two instruments do Claudius and Laertes plan to kill Hamlet?

____

9. What happens to Ophelia at the end of this act?

____

10. What reason does Claudius give Laertes for not punishing Hamlet for Polonius' death?

____

Short Answer Quiz Key

1. Polonius' body.
2. The execution of Hamlet.
3. Fortinbras' army.
4. It drives her insane.
5. Laertes returns from France, and charges into the castle at the head of a mob, demanding satisfaction for his father's death.
6. He is captured by pirates.
7. A small piece of land that has been claimed by Poland.
8. A sharp, poisoned foil, and a poisoned chalice.
9. She drowns in a nearby river.
10. He explains that he could not punish Hamlet because Hamlet is too beloved by his mother and by the common people.

Day 4 - Crossword Puzzle

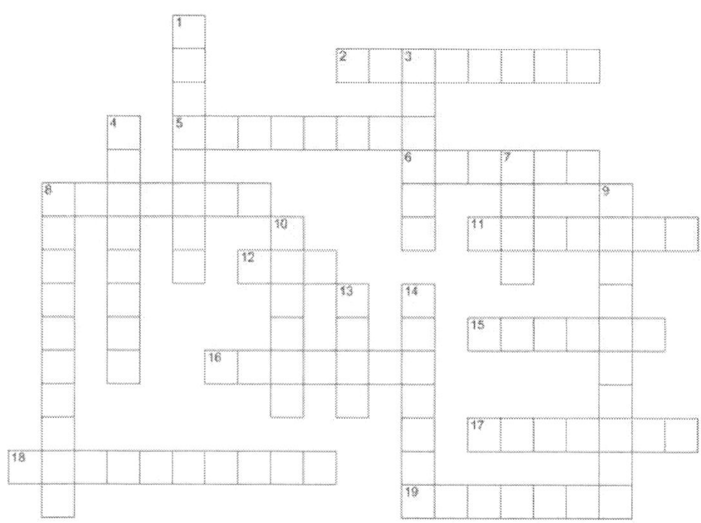

ACROSS

2. angry
5. brings news of Ophelia's fate
6. mob of commoners
8. Ophelia's tokens
11. Laertes' talent
12. before (archaic)
15. clothing
16. mob's choice for king
17. Hamlet's captors
18. sorrows come in these, according to Claudius
19. Hamlet's destination

DOWN

1. royal procession
3. angel
4. Ophelia's fate
7. platform for a corpse
8. marching against Poland
9. mentally distressed
10. cowardly
13. sanity (plural)
14. hidden

Crossword Puzzle Answer Key

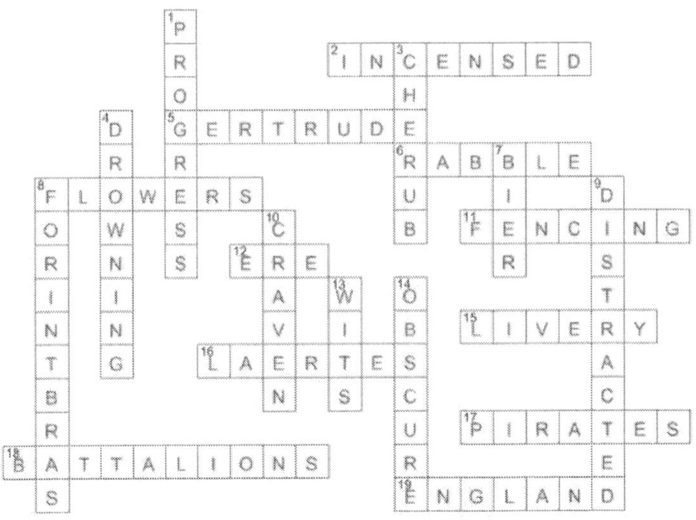

ACROSS

2. angry
5. brings news of Ophelia's fate
6. mob of commoners
8. Ophelia's tokens
11. Laertes' talent
12. before (archaic)
15. clothing
16. mob's choice for king
17. Hamlet's captors
18. sorrows come in these, according to Claudius
19. Hamlet's destination

DOWN

1. royal procession
3. angel
4. Ophelia's fate
7. platform for a corpse
8. marching against Poland
9. mentally distressed
10. cowardly
13. sanity (plural)
14. hidden

Day 4 - Vocabulary Quiz

Terms		Answers
1. ____	Pith	A. admit; tolerate
2. ____	Countenance	B. persistent; unyielding
3. ____	Compound	C. extra; more than what is necessary
4. ____	Convocation	D. position or entrench troops
5. ____	Bark	E. cowardly
6. ____	Garrison	F. ship; vessel
7. ____	Craven	G. assumption; speculation
8. ____	Importunate	H. willingly, eagerly
9. ____	Conjecture	I. costume; uniform
10. ____	Superfluous	J. hidden; concealed
11. ____	Rabble	K. gathering
12. ____	Obscure	L. angry, disorderly mob
13. ____	Livery	M. innermost core; essence
14. ____	Foil	N. mix; combine to form a whole.
15. ____	Fain	O. thin sword used in fencing

Vocabulary Quiz Answer Key

1. M
2. A
3. N
4. K
5. F
6. D
7. E
8. B
9. G
10. C
11. L
12. J
13. I
14. O
15. H

Day 4 - Classroom Activities

1. Suicide in Hamlet

   Kind of Activity: Individual Writing
   Objective: Students will demonstrate an ability to support an assertion by citing specific textual evidence.
   Common Core State Standards: CCSS.ELA-Literacy.RL.11-12.1
   Time: 45-60 min. (You can save class time by assigning prep work for homework)

   Structure:

   The true nature of Ophelia's death in Act IV is one of the unsolved "mysteries" in *Hamlet* - was it an accident, or was it suicide?

   The specter of suicide hangs over most of the action of *Hamlet*. Hamlet expresses suicidal thoughts a mere four lines into his first soliloquy in Act I, and suicide is the focus of his "To be or not to be" speech in Act III. As with the case of Ophelia's death, the issue of whether these suicidal thoughts are genuine is the subject of some debate.

   This activity will involve a written assignment in which students will attempt to resolve this debate. The Mayo Clinic web site provides a comprehensive list of the symptoms of suicidal behavior: http://www.mayoclinic.com/health/suicide/DS01062/DSECTION=symptoms. The students' task will be to link as many of these symptoms as possible to specific lines or incidents in the text to support their interpretations.

   Ideans for Differentiated Instruction: While this is primarily a written assignment, you can open this topic up to a general class discussion once the assignment has been completed.

   Assessment Ideas:
   As a creative writing assignment, have students write "letters" to Hamlet or Ophelia (or, alternatively, Claudius, Gertrude, Polonius, or Horatio) in which they express their concerns over each character's behavior. In this letter, students should cite specific scenes from the text, and should allude to the selected reference material regarding suicide.

2. Perspective in Hamlet

   Kind of Activity: Creative Writing

Objective: Student will demonstrate how point of view or purpose shapes the content and style of a text.
Common Core State Standards: CCSS.ELA-Literacy.RL.11-12.6
Time: 45-60 min. (You can save class time by assigning prep work for homework)

Structure:

By way of introduction, you can show students a scene from Stoppard's *Rosencrantz and Guildenstern Are Dead* to show how a different perspective on a scene encourages a completely different interpretation of its meaning. The scene depicting Hamlet's first meeting with the pair, for example, shows how without the benefit of Hamlet's soliloquies, his actions do indeed look like those of a madman.

Have each student pick a secondary character from the play (e.g. Horatio, Ophelia, Fortinbras, Polonius, etc - give students free reign to be creative) and have them rewrite a key scene from this character's perspective. For example, how would the play-within-a-play come across from Ophelia's perspective? Students can feel free to add new details based on what we already know of these characters, but their stories should still be grounded in a close reading of the existing text. The main goal of this exercise is for students to show how the withholding of key pieces of information affects the way a scene can be interpreted.

Ideans for Differentiated Instruction: If your class lacks experienced of enthusiastic creative writers, you can change the focus of the assignment to more of an analysis of a scene: have students describe how the point of reference of a scene affects the way the audience interprets its action.

Assessment Ideas:
As a follow-up group activity, you can encourage students to "combine" their character sketches into a new, collectively authored scene, and have students give live or filmed presentations of these scenes.

Day 5 - Reading Assignment

Read Act V.

Common Core Objectives

- CCSS.ELA-Literacy.CCRA.L.3 Apply knowledge of language to understand how language functions in different contexts, to make effective choices for meaning or style, and to comprehend more fully when reading or listening.
- CCSS.ELA-Literacy.CCRA.L.4 Determine or clarify the meaning of unknown and multiple-meaning words and phrases by using context clues, analyzing meaningful word parts, and consulting general and specialized reference materials, as appropriate.
- CCSS.ELA-Literacy.CCRA.L.5 Demonstrate understanding of figurative language, word relationships, and nuances in word meanings.
- CCSS.ELA-Literacy.CCRA.R.1 Read closely to determine what the text says explicitly and to make logical inferences from it; cite specific textual evidence when writing or speaking to support conclusions drawn from the text.
- CCSS.ELA-Literacy.CCRA.W.1 Write arguments to support claims in an analysis of substantive topics or texts using valid reasoning and relevant and sufficient evidence.

Note that it is perfectly fine to expand any day's work into two days depending on the characteristics of the class, particularly if the class will engage in all of the suggested classroom exercises and activities and discuss all of the thought questions.

Content Summary for Teachers

Act V:

Act V opens on a graveyard outside Elsinore, where a sexton and his assistant (referred to as "clowns" in the text) are digging a new grave. Hamlet, returning to Elsinore with Horatio, comes upon the sexton as he tosses aside old bones to make room for a new arrival. The pair is amused by the gallows humor with which the sexton plies his trade, but Hamlet's mood becomes more contemplative when the sexton unearths the skull of Yorick, who was the king's jester when Hamlet was a small child. Seeing an approaching funeral procession headed by the king, Hamlet and Horatio hide themselves. Hearing Laertes' lamentations, Hamlet realizes that it is Ophelia's funeral he is watching, and leaps forward to voice his own greater grief. After a brief scuffle, Laertes and Hamlet are separated from one another.

Back at Elsinore, Hamlet explains to Horatio how he uncovered Claudius' plot to have him executed, and how he forged a new letter calling for the deaths of

Rosencrantz and Guildenstern. Their conversation is interrupted by Osric, a sycophantic courtier, who enters with news of the proposed duel with Laertes. Despite Horatio's warning against it, Hamlet accepts.

The stage is soon set for the duel, and the royal entourage enters. After Hamlet and Laertes exchange rather forced courtesies, the match begins. Hamlet scores the first two points, after which Claudius offers him the poisoned chalice. When Hamlet refuses the cup, it is taken up by Gertrude, who offers a toast to her son and drinks from it. After Hamlet scores yet another point, a frustrated Laertes wounds him with his poisoned sword. A fight breaks out between the two, and in the scuffle, Laertes is stabbed with his own poisoned blade. As Claudius tries to calm the melee, Gertrude falls, and as she dies, she announces that she has been poisoned. Laertes, also dying, turns on Claudius and reveals the poison plot to Hamlet, and begs his forgiveness. Hamlet finally attacks Claudius, stabbing him with the poisoned sword, and forcing the poisoned wine down his throat for good measure. Before he himself dies, Hamlet asks Horatio to tell his tale.

Just then, the sound of drums announces the arrival of Fortinbras. A group of English ambassadors accompany him, bringing word of the deaths of Rosencrantz and Guildenstern. As the last man standing, and with Hamlet's dying approval, Fortinbras assumes the Danish crown, and promises a soldier's funeral for the dead prince.

Thought Questions (students consider while they read)

1. Why do you think Shakespeare inserts the comic interaction between the gravediggers right before Ophelia's funeral?
2. What do we learn about Gertrude's plans for Hamlet and Gertrude in scene 1? How does this contradict what we learned about their relationship in Act I?
3. How does Hamlet's mood change after his encounter with the pirates?
4. The character of Osric is a caricature of the ideal of the courtier, or the Renaissance version of a politician/bureaucrat. How might his character be a commentary on the nature of politics?
5. In the end, did Hamlet really get his revenge?

Vocabulary (in order of appearance)

Sc. i, l. 140:

- Equivocation: verbal ambiguity

Sc. i, l. 163:

- Sexton: church caretaker

Sc. i, l. 189:

- Gorge: the contents of the stomach

Sc. i, l. 191:

- Gambol: to dance or jump around merrily

Sc. i, l. 215:

- Imperious: domineering

Sc. i, l. 228:

- Obsequies: funeral rites

Sc. i, l. 238:

- Requiem: a hymn asking for rest for the dead

Sc. i, l. 242:

- Churlish: rude, surly

Sc. i, l. 266:

- Asunder: apart

Sc. i, l. 275:

- Forbear: restrain

Sc. ii, l. 73:

- Interim: the time in between two events

Sc. ii, l. 92:

- Impart: convey; communicate

Sc. ii, l. 111:

- Gentry: people of noble birth

Sc. ii, l. 117:

- Extolment: praise

Sc. ii, l. 159:

- Germane: pertinent; relevant

Sc. ii, l. 230:

- Distraction: mental disorder or distress

Additional Homework

1. If Ophelia's death were really a suicide, why would that mean that she would have to be denied certain funeral rites? Research Medieval and Renaissance views on suicide. Why was it considered such a grave sin?

Day 5 - Discussion of Thought Questions

1. Why do you think Shakespeare inserts the comic interaction between the gravediggers right before Ophelia's funeral?

   Time: 5 min.

   Discussion: Responses will vary. As with any instance of comic relief, the primary purpose of the gravediggers is to break the unrelenting gloom of the previous scenes, and to provide a respite before the heartbreaking spectacle of Ophelia's funeral. In other sense, the gravedigger scene also allows for a different perspective on one of the play's main themes - death.

2. What do we learn about Gertrude's plans for Hamlet and Gertrude in scene 1? How does this contradict what we learned about their relationship in Act I?

   Time: 5 min.

   Discussion: In the burial scene, we learn that Gertrude had intended for Ophelia to be Hamlet's bride. This contradicts what we learn in Act I, in which Laertes insists that, because of Hamlet's status as prince, he and Ophelia could never be married.

3. How does Hamlet's mood change after his encounter with the pirates?

   Time: 5 min.

   Discussion: When we last saw Hamlet in Act IV, he was a raging loose cannon. In Act V, we are presented with a more sober, subdued Hamlet. Hamlet's serendipitous capture seems to have renewed his faith in divine providence. The Hamlet of the previous acts chided himself for his inability to act, but this new Hamlet seems resigned him to whatever fate might have in store for him.

4. The character of Osric is a caricature of the ideal of the courtier, or the Renaissance version of a politician/bureaucrat. How might his character be a commentary on the nature of politics?

   Time: 5 min.

   Discussion: Ridiculed by Hamlet and Horatio, Osric is meant to demonstrate the silliness and superficiality of the political life.

5. In the end, did Hamlet really get his revenge?

   Time: 5 min.

   Discussion: On the surface, Hamlet does get his revenge by killing Claudius, and by doing so in a way that does not force him to compromise himself morally (as Laertes does). At the same time, Hamlet's revenge inflicts a great deal of collateral damage; Polonius, Ophelia, Gertrude, and Laertes are also, in a sense, victims of his revenge. So, while it might be possible to view Hamlet's killing of Claudius a victory, it is a pyrrhic one at best.

Day 5 - Short Answer Quiz

1. Where does scene 1 take place?

____

2. Who is Yorick?

____

3. Why is Ophelia denied an ordinary funeral?

____

4. Based on the way he is treated by Hamlet and Horatio, what kind of character is Osric?

____

5. How did Hamlet thwart Claudius' first attempt to have him killed?

____

6. Before it is interrupted, who is winning the fencing match between Hamlet and Laertes?

____

7. How does Claudius' plan to use a poisoned chalice backfire?

8. How Laertes' plan backfire?

9. What happens to Rosencrantz and Guildenstern when they reach England?

10. Who will be the next king of Denmark?

Short Answer Quiz Key

1. In a graveyard outside Elsinore Castle.
2. Yorick is the king's long dead jester, whose skull is exhumed by the gravedigger.
3. Because the circumstances of her death are in question; it's possible she could have committed suicide.
4. Osric is a pretentious and simpering sycophant.
5. By intercepting Claudius' letter and replacing it with his own forgery, which ordered the immediate deaths of Rosencrantz and Guildenstern on their arrival in England.
6. Hamlet
7. Hamlet refuses the chalice, and Gertrude drinks from it instead.
8. While scuffling, Hamlet and Laertes accidentally switch swords, and Laertes is wounded by his own poisoned sword.
9. They are executed.
10. Fortinbras

Day 5 - Crossword Puzzle

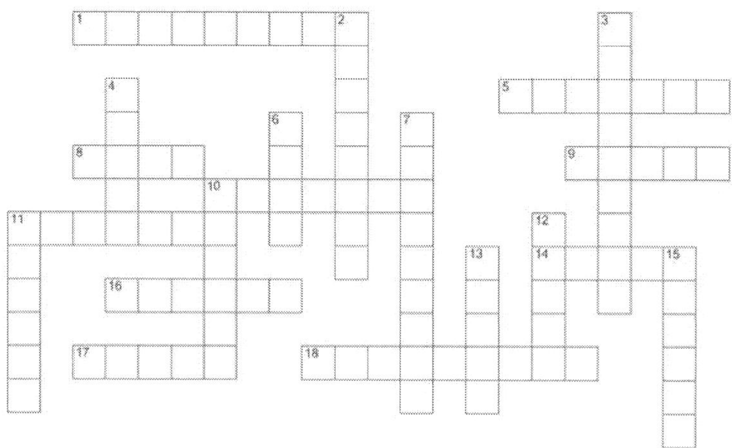

ACROSS

1. poisoned
5. lives to tell the tale
8. pay attention
9. awaits Rosencrantz and Guildenstern in England
10. Ophelia's death is rumored to be this
11. Hamlet's last words: "The rest is ________"
14. foolish courtier
16. Yorick's profession
17. comedic character in Elizabethan drama
18. funeral rites

DOWN

2. "There's a ________ that shapes our ends"
3. setting of scene 1
4. villain
6. fencing sword
7. famous Greek conqueror
10. church officer
11. gravedigger's refuse
12. stomach contents (n.); to eat voraciously (v.)
13. tankard, stein
15. sore, ulcer

Crossword Puzzle Answer Key

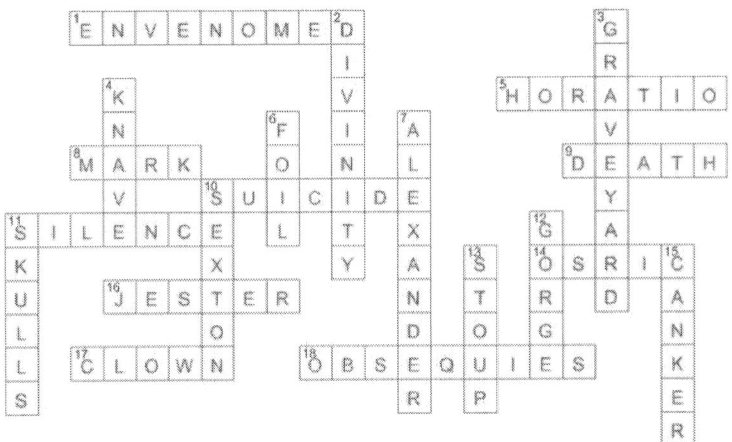

ACROSS

1. poisoned
5. lives to tell the tale
8. pay attention
9. awaits Rosencrantz and Guildenstern in England
10. Ophelia's death is rumored to be this
11. Hamlet's last words: "The rest is ________."
14. foolish courtier
16. Yorick's profession
17. comedic character in Elizabethan drama
18. funeral rites

DOWN

2. "There's a ________ that shapes our ends"
3. setting of scene 1
4. villain
6. fencing sword
7. famous Greek conqueror
10. church officer
11. gravedigger's refuse
12. stomach contents (n.); to eat voraciously (v.)
13. tankard, stein
15. sore, ulcer

Day 5 - Vocabulary Quiz

Terms	Answers
1. ____ Equivocation	A. rude, surly
2. ____ Sexton	B. verbal ambiguity
3. ____ Gorge	C. mental disorder or distress
4. ____ Gambol	D. to dance or jump around merrily
5. ____ Imperious	E. convey; communicate
6. ____ Obsequies	F. praise
7. ____ Requiem	G. pertinent; relevant
8. ____ Churlish	H. a hymn requesting for rest for the dead
9. ____ Asunder	I. restrain
10. ____ Forbear	J. the contents of the stomach
11. ____ Interim	K. funeral rites
12. ____ Impart	L. people of noble birth
13. ____ Gentry	M. the time in between two events
14. ____ Extolment	N. apart
15. ____ Germane	O. domineering
16. ____ Distraction	P. church caretaker

Vocabulary Quiz Answer Key

1. B
2. P
3. J
4. D
5. O
6. K
7. H
8. A
9. N
10. I
11. M
12. E
13. L
14. F
15. G
16. C

Day 5 - Classroom Activities

1. Shakespeare in Your Own Words

   Kind of Activity: Collaborative Writing
   Objective: Students will demonstrate an understanding of complex vocabulary, and will develop an appreciation for sophisticated rhetorical devices.
   Common Core State Standards: CCSS.ELA-Literacy.L.11-12.3, CCSS.ELA-Literacy.L.11-12.4, CCSS.ELA-Literacy.L.11-12.5
   Time: 45-60 min. (You can save class time by assigning prep work for homework)

   Structure:

   The purpose of this activity is to have students demonstrate that they can recount what they have read in *Hamlet* in modern, "un-Shakespearean" language. As a comic way of introducing this activity, show students the parody of Hamlet's graveyard scene from the cartoon *Animaniacs* (available at: http://www.youtube.com/watch?v=Mtz7IwgQvNc) or, if the technology is not available, have them read Prince Charles' modern rewording of the "To be or not to be" speech (available at: http://articles.latimes.com/1990-02-13/news/vw-472_1_prince-charles).

   Break your class up into groups of 3-4 students. (You should assign these groups; highly proficient students should provide guidance to students who might be struggling with the material.) Assign each group a significant scene from the play, and have them rewrite it in a modern setting using modern languages. Students can, following the *Animaniacs* model, taking an irreverent approach to the material, but whatever their interpretation, it should have a firm grounding in and direct connection to the original text.

   Once students have handed in or presented their scenes, lead a class discussion in which students share their experiences "translating" Shakespeare's language. What was their reaction to the material when they read or heard it in contemporary language? Along with making sure that students are able to decipher text at this most sophisticated level, the point of this exercise is to help students gain an appreciation of how the power of a literary work often lies in the beauty of its rhetoric.

   Ideans for Differentiated Instruction: Depending on the size of your class, you can also assign this as an independent writing assignment. If your class has a number of extroverts or experienced actors, you can encourage them to act out the scene they have written before class, or, if the technology is available, in a video presentation.

Assessment Ideas:
As a counterpoint to this lesson, have students take a scene from a modern film, play, of TV show, and rewrite it in Shakespearean language, referencing the language, idioms, and grammar constructs used in *Hamlet*. If the space, time, and technology allow, encourage students to present these scenes in a live or video format.

2. The Great Debate

Kind of Activity: Group Work
Objective: Students will demonstrate an understanding of what text explicitly says, and also what can be inferred from it. Students will also demonstrate an ability to analyze complex characters.
Common Core State Standards: CCSS.ELA-Literacy.RL.11-12.1, CCSS.ELA-Literacy.W.11-12.1,
Time: 45-60 min.

Structure:

Now that we have reached the end of *Hamlet*, we have been presented with four examples of leadership: Old Hamlet and Claudius (both of whom were kings), Hamlet (who would have been king), and Fortinbras (who will be king).

Ask students to envision an election in which the characters are running for the "office" of king. Based on what we have read, which one of these characters would make the best king? Divide you class into small groups, and assign one of these kings to each. Depending on the size of your class, feel free to add "dark horse" candidates - that is, candidates who would not normally be in a position of real power in the world of *Hamlet* (e.g. Ophelia, Gertrude, Horatio, Laertes). Each group will develop the platform for each character, pointing out their own character's strength, and the other character's faults.

The purpose of this activity is twofold: 1) to test each student's ability to support claims about a character through a close reading of a text, and 2) to demonstrate that characters can be far more complex and nuanced than the normal categories of "good" and "evil" might suggest.

Ideans for Differentiated Instruction: Depending on the size of the class and the time available, this activity can be performed as an actual classroom team debate, or handed in as a written assignment.

Assessment Ideas:

Once all of the arguments for each "candidate" have been put forth, have students create a graph or chart (or, if the technology allows, a multimedia presentation) outlining each character's strengths and weaknesses.

Final Paper

Essay Questions

1. *Hamlet* has been described as a "tragedy of a man who could not make up his mind." Do you feel this is an accurate portrayal of Hamlet? Is Hamlet's revenge delayed by his own indecision, or is he merely the victim of forces and circumstances beyond his control? Cite specific evidence from the text to justify your reasoning.

2. Did Hamlet genuinely love Ophelia? And what of Ophelia – did she sincerely love Hamlet? What was the true nature of their relationship – platonic, or romantic/sexual? Cite specific evidence from the text to justify your reasoning.

3. Hamlet, Laertes, and Fortinbras are characters with a common bond: each is a son seeking revenge for a murdered father. How do their approaches to achieving this revenge differ? Which character, if any, has the most admirable approach? Or the most effective? Cite specific evidence from the text to justify your reasoning.

4. Comment on the nature of the ghost. Is it good ("a spirit of health") or evil (a "goblin damned")? Is the ghost even real? Cite specific evidence from the text to support your argument.

5. At times throughout the play, Hamlet expresses a rather low opinion of women. How do the female characters of *Hamlet* subvert his views? Cite specific evidence from the text to support your view.

6. Think about the role that theater plays in *Hamlet*. What does this say about the nature of theater and drama? Conversely, what might it say about reality?

7. A hero is normally defined as a character who serves as a model of bravery, self-sacrifice, and virtue. Based on this definition, who do you think is the "hero" of *Hamlet*?

Advice on research sources

A. School or community library

Ask your reference librarian for help locating books on the following subjects:

* Shakespeare and his influence on Wesern literature

* *Hamlet*

* Literary criticism

* Revenge in literature

* Dramatic representations of madness

* Women in the Renaissance

* Renaissance cosmology / views of the afterlife

B. Other dramatic work

Thematically relevant work to consider include the Shakespeare plays *Macbeth*, *Julius Caesar*, and *The Tempest*.

Grading rubric for essays

Style:

* words: spelling and diction

* sentences: grammar and punctuation

* paragraphs: organization

* essay: structure

* argument: rhetoric, reasonableness, creativity

Content:

* accuracy

* use of evidence

* addresses the question

* completeness

* uses literary concepts

* addresses complex and sensitive subjects with understanding and nuance

Final Paper Answer Key

Remember that essays about literature should not be graded with a cookie-cutter approach whereby specific words or ideas are required. See the grading rubric above for a variety of criteria to use in assessing answers to the essay questions. This answer key thus functions as a store of ideas for students who need additional guidance in framing their answers.

1. *Hamlet* has been described as a "tragedy of a man who could not make up his mind." Do you feel this is an accurate portrayal of Hamlet? Is Hamlet's revenge delayed by his own indecision, or is he merely the victim of forces and circumstances beyond his control? Cite specific evidence from the text to justify your reasoning.

   Responses will vary. Students who take up the position that Hamlet is indeed indecisive must account for his impulsive murder of Polonius, who Hamlet believed to be Claudius. They must also explain why Hamlet's metaphysical doubts (i.e. about the ghost's true nature, or about Claudius' fate if he is murdered while praying) are unreasonable. On the other side, students who argue against Hamlet's being indecisive must explain his repeated delays. Throughout the play, Hamlet chides himself for his inaction and resolves to act as he knows he should, only to take up some new distraction in the scenes that follow.

2. Did Hamlet genuinely love Ophelia? And what of Ophelia – did she sincerely love Hamlet? What was the true nature of their relationship – platonic, or romantic/sexual? Cite specific evidence from the text to justify your reasoning.

   Responses will vary. A correct student response should note that the bawdy songs sung by Ophelia after her mental collapse hint at a previous sexual relationship with Hamlet, though the extent or length of that relationship is never really made clear. Whatever its sexual component, it is clear that their relationship was more than platonic. Students who take the view that Hamlet did not love Ophelia must account for his outsized grief at her funeral, where he claims to have loved her more than "forty thousand brothers." Students who argue that Hamlet did indeed love Ophelia must explain his unprovoked cruelty in Act III; it is possible that this behavior is just a part of the "antic disposition" he is using to cover his knowledge of Claudius' crimes.

3. Hamlet, Laertes, and Fortinbras are characters with a common bond: each is a son seeking revenge for a murdered father. How do their approaches to achieving this revenge differ? Which character, if any, has the most admirable approach? Or the most effective? Cite specific evidence from the text to justify your reasoning.

Responses will vary, but correct student responses should mention the following: Hamlet's approach to revenge could best be described as circuitous - he is first hindered by doubt and self-recrimination, then by Claudius' attempts to have him murdered. In the end, Hamlet has his revenge, but it comes at the cost of several innocent lives, including his own. Laertes, on the other hand, pursues his revenge with hot-headed abandon, literally knocking down doors to avenge his father's death. He, too, gets his revenge, but since he must debase himself by resorting to deception and allying himself with the villainous Claudius, it is ultimately a hollow victory. While Fortinbras' attempts at revenge are stifled, he is able to derive some sort of satisfaction from his military conquests, but as Hamlet points out, his quest for glory comes at the price of thousands of innocent lives.

4. Comment on the nature of the ghost. Is it good ("a spirit of health") or evil (a "goblin damned")? Is the ghost even real? Cite specific evidence from the text to support your argument.

   Responses will vary, but student responses should comment on the following: Students who argue that the ghost is benevolent must account for the fact that it is asking Hamlet to commit murder. Those who argue that the ghost is some sort of demon should explain why he urges Hamlet not to be angry with his mother. If students argue that the ghost is real, they must somehow explain how it is that Gertrude isn't able to see it, while those who feel it is not real must account for the fact that Hamlet, Horatio, Marcellus, and Bernardo *are* able to see it.

5. At times throughout the play, Hamlet expresses a rather low opinion of women. How do the female characters of *Hamlet* subvert his views? Cite specific evidence from the text to support your view.

   A student response should note: In spite of Hamlet's view of women as faithless and fickle, Gertrude and Ophelia are some of the most loyal and faithful characters in *Hamlet*. Ophelia is obedient to her father and brother almost to a fault, and her grief when she believes she is the cause of Hamlet's mental distress seems genuine. We know little of Gertrude's exact role in Old Hamlet's death, but from we see of her in the play, he appears to be a sincerely affectionate and caring mother, and a faithful wife.

6. Think about the role that theater plays in *Hamlet*. What does this say about the nature of theater and drama? Conversely, what might it say about reality?

   Responses will vary, but student responses should include a thorough discussion of the arrival of the traveling players and Hamlet's interaction with them, and the subsequent play-within-a-play. Hamlet's soliloquy following his encounter with the players is a commentary on the power of theater to use imagination to convey and provoke genuine emotional reactions. The play-within-a-play that follows demonstrates this power when it cracks the carefully-constructed persona that Claudius has created to hide his crimes. One of the messages of *Hamlet* seems to be that in its ability to strike at the heart of human truths, there is something more "real" about theater than reality itself.

7. A hero is normally defined as a character who serves as a model of bravery, self-sacrifice, and virtue. Based on this definition, who do you think is the "hero" of *Hamlet*?

   Responses will vary. Students who choose Hamlet himself should address how he can be considered a hero in spite of his moral failings, such as his cruelty to Ophelia, his inability to act, his reckless killing of Polonius. A more plausible character might be Horatio. Against the tableau of villains and flawed characters who inhabit the world of *Hamlet*, Horatio stands as a model of loyalty, kindness, and honesty. Another plausible choice would be Ophelia who, unlike most of the other characters in the play, does not commit some sort of crime against another character (this is also true of Horatio). Throughout the play, she is a model of loyalty and self-sacrifice, and even in her madness there is an innocence and gentleness that is touching. Students may also respond that, in the morally complex world of *Hamlet*, there are no true heroes. In these responses, students should point out how each character falls short of the heroic ideal.

Final Exam

A. Multiple Choice

Circle the letter corresponding to the best answer.

1. As the play begins, Elsinore is preparing for war with

   (A) Norway
   (B) England
   (C) Denmark
   (D) France

2. Horatio is Hamlet's

   (A) schoolmate
   (B) cousin
   (C) liege
   (D) servant

3. Read the following lines from Act I: "But I have that within which passeth show / These but the trappings and the suits of woe." These lines touch upon the play's theme of

   (A) madness
   (B) revenge
   (C) appearance vs. reality
   (D) man vs. supernatural

4. At the end of Act I, Hamlet asks his companions to swear to

   (A) allow him to accompany them on their watch
   (B) deny Claudius' marriage to Gertrude
   (C) avenge his father's murder
   (D) not reveal what they have seen

5. In Act II, Claudius is preoccupied with

   (A) identifying the cause of Hamlet's behavior
   (B) marrying Gertrude
   (C) defeating Fortinbras
   (D) finding Polonius' body

6. Ophelia's encounter with Hamlet in her chamber can best be described as

(A) romantic
(B) joyous
(C) bizarre
(D) violent

7. According to the conversation between Hamlet, Rosencrantz, and Guildenstern in Act II, Denmark has been overrun by

(A) refugees
(B) soldiers
(C) bandits
(D) child actors

8. In his soliloquy at the end of Act II, Hamlet compares

(A) an actor's motivation to his own
(B) Rosencrantz and Guildenstern to Horatio
(C) Claudius to his father
(D) his desire for revenge to Fortinbras'

9. According to Hamlet's "To be or not to be" speech, which of the following makes death such a frightening prospect?

(A) "The native hue of resolution"
(B) "What dreams may come"
(C) "Th' oppressor's wrong"
(D) "The slings and arrows of outrageous fortune"

10. Hamlet most admires Horatio for his

(A) intelligence
(B) stoicism
(C) sense of humor
(D) passion

11. Act III marks the first time Claudius expresses

(A) affection
(B) gratitude
(C) remorse
(D) curiosity

12. The considerations prevent Hamlet from killing Claudius when he has the opportunity could best be described as

(A) supernatural
(B) legal
(C) practical
(D) political

13. When Hamlet kills Polonius, he does so because

(A) he is angered by Polonius' eavesdropping
(B) he wants to frighten his mother
(C) he mistakes Polonius for Claudius
(D) he is following the ghost's command

14. At the close of Act III, Hamlet urges his mother to

(A) watch over Ophelia
(B) hide Polonius' body
(C) beware of the ghost
(D) reject Claudius' advances

15. In Act IV, Claudius' guards are overtaken by a mob led by

(A) Laertes
(B) Osric
(C) Voltemand
(D) Fortinbras

16. In her madness, Ophelia often expresses herself by

    (A) miming
    (B) quoting Bible verses
    (C) making riddles
    (D) singing

17. Which of the following best characterizes the change in Hamlet's mood from Act IV to Act V?

    (A) from anger to acceptance
    (B) from fear to determination
    (C) from defeat to triumph
    (D) from doubt to resolution

18. Hamlet and Horatio's attitude toward Osric could best be described as

    (A) compassion
    (B) reverence
    (C) suspicion
    (D) ridicule

19. Aside from poison, what is another advantage Laertes has in his duel with Hamlet?

    (A) armor under his clothes
    (B) a sharpened blade
    (C) a biased referee
    (D) a dagger hidden in his boot

20. Which of the following would most likely occur immediately after the final scene of *Hamlet*?

    (A) a wedding
    (B) a funeral
    (C) a battle
    (D) a coronation

B. Short Answer

1. When did Old Hamlet defeat Old Fortinbras?

2. Who are the only major characters to survive Act 5?

3. When Horatio and the guards encounter the ghost, what is the ghost wearing?

4. According to his soliloquy in Act 3, why is it impossible for Claudius to fully repent his crimes?

5. Why do Marcellus and Bernardo think Horatio is better qualified to speak to the ghost than they are?

6. What act is Hamlet contemplating in his "To be or not to be" speech?

7. Aside from Norway, what other country has Denmark defeated before the action of *Hamlet*?

8. According to Gertrude's explanation, what was it that dragged Ophelia underwater, drowning her?

9. Before he learns of Claudius' treachery, who is the main target of Hamlet's resentment?

10. What kind of funeral does Fortinbras plan for Hamlet?

C. Vocabulary

Terms

1. ____ Equivocation
2. ____ Imperious
3. ____ Asunder
4. ____ Germane
5. ____ Countenance
6. ____ Craven
7. ____ Superfluous
8. ____ Convocation
9. ____ Visage
10. ____ Vouchsafe
11. ____ Fetters
12. ____ Discourse
13. ____ Wonted
14. ____ Malefaction
15. ____ Slander
16. ____ Firmament
17. ____ Obsequious
18. ____ Circumscribed
19. ____ Enmity
20. ____ Mettle

Answers

A. face
B. courage; resilience
C. verbal ambiguity
D. conversation, communication, intellectual exchange
E. related to obsequies (funerals); excessively obedient or servile
F. extra; more than what is necessary
G. pertinent; relevant
H. mutual ill will; hatred
I. crime, misdeed
J. cowardly
K. give, offer, grant
L. defamation; false statements intended to damage a person's reputation
M. set within particular limits
N. apart
O. sky
P. gathering
Q. domineering
R. customary, usual
S. chains, shackles, restraints
T. admit; tolerate

D. Short Essays

1. Consider the advice that Polonius gives Laertes before he returns to school in France. How is this advice ironic, especially coming from Polonius?

2. How is Ophelia's response to the loss of her father different from that of Hamlet's or Laertes'? What do you think this says about the position of women in the world of *Hamlet*?

3. *Hamlet* features a number of scenes in which a character or characters observe the actions of other characters in secret. How does this heighten the dramatic tension of the play?

Final Exam Answer Key

A. Multiple Choice Answer Key

1. A
2. A
3. C
4. D
5. A
6. C
7. D
8. A
9. B
10. B
11. C
12. A
13. C
14. D
15. A
16. D
17. A
18. D
19. B
20. B

B. Short Answer Key

1. On the day Hamlet was born
2. Horatio and Fortinbras
3. Armor
4. Because he cannot give up what he has gained from committing them.
5. Because Horatio is "a scholar."
6. Suicide
7. England
8. Her gown
9. Gertrude
10. A soldier's funeral

C. Vocabulary Answer Key

1. C
2. Q
3. N
4. G
5. T
6. J
7. F
8. P
9. A
10. K
11. S
12. D
13. R
14. I
15. L
16. O
17. E
18. M
19. H
20. B

D. Short Essays Answer Key

1. Before Laertes departs for France, Polonius advises him that above all else, he must be true to himself. This is ironic on two levels. First, this advice comes at the end of a long list of instructions Polonius gives Laertes about how he should comport himself in public, all of which seem to go against the idea of Laertes being true to himself. More ironic than this is the fact that this advice is coming from Polonius, who is himself something of a weathervane. Judging from Polonius' scheming behavior in the remainder of the play, it is difficult to think of him being "true" to himself. In fact, given the way he shapes himself according to his audience, it's hard to say whether Polonius has any true "self" at all.
2. When confronted by the loss of their fathers, Hamlet and Laertes both respond with rage and oaths of revenge, though the paths they take to achieve this revenge are quite different from one another. Ophelia, constrained by the limits placed on women in the male-dominated world of

Hamlet, has no such recourse to action. With no options available to her and no one left to turn to, her only recourse is madness and, ultimately, death.

3. The fact that certain characters monitor the actions of other characters in secret increases the tension of the play because it heightens the audience's expectation of what it knows is imminent. For example, when Hamlet stages his play in Act III, the audience is aware that he is doing so in order to secretly monitor Claudius' reaction to the play, though Claudius himself is unaware of this. This scene is made more tense, then, because we know that stakes of the scene are higher than the characters participating in it realize.

Lesson Plans

GradeSaver™

Getting you the grade since 1999™

Other Lesson Plans from GradeSaver™

The Adventures of Huckleberry Finn
Animal Farm
The Book Thief
Brave New World
The Canterbury Tales
Death of a Salesman
Emily Dickinson's Collected Poems
Fahrenheit 451
The Great Gatsby
Gulliver's Travels
Hamlet
Heart of Darkness
Into the Wild
The Kite Runner
Life of Pi
Lord of the Flies
Macbeth
Oedipus Rex or Oedipus the King
Of Mice and Men
Poe's Poetry
The Scarlet Letter
A Streetcar Named Desire
To Kill a Mockingbird
The Yellow Wallpaper

Made in the USA
Lexington, KY
20 November 2014